Never Too Late

Teaching Adults to Read & Write

Diana Hanbury King

Never Too Late. Diana Hanbury King. WVCED.com.

International Standard Book Number: 978-1-945998-00-3.

Cover design by Steve Bowers. To purchase additional copies, visit wvced.com.

Dedication

For Wayne LaMade, who had the courage to let me teach him many years ago when I was young and inexperienced. He has gone on to do many important things with his life, including the presidency of the Indiana Branch of the International Dyslexia Association. He runs a successful business and has raised wonderful family.

Table of Contents

Never Too Late. Diana Hanbury King. WVCED.com.

Introduction

"When I was in school, I wondered why I didn't get it. Now I wonder why they didn't get it." Colin

Teaching an adult is not like teaching a child. When we teach children, we begin with short vowels and single consonants, introduced one at a time. Working with adults is different. In the course of their life experience, they are likely to have picked up some sight words and may even have figured out some of the vowel and consonant combinations.

We have to work in two directions. First of all, we must fill any gaps in their knowledge of the basics. For instance, they may not know the principle that governs the sounds of c and g, their knowledge of the vowel teams is likely to be spotty, and they may not even be aware of silent-e syllables.

At the same time we should be working on morphology, on the prefixes, roots, and suffixes that form Latin-based words and the elements that comprise the Greek. These are relatively phonetic.

Begin by explaining the following to your student.

English is a complicated language because when you are learning English you are actually learning three separate languages, each of which has its own system.

First, there are the Anglo-Saxon, or Germanic words. These are the oldest words in the language. They tend to be short words and names for common things such as body parts, domestic animals, numbers and colors, and common verbs. Unfortunately, they are also the most irregular words in English, often with silent letters and difficult vowel teams.

Never Too Late. Diana Hanbury King. WVCED.com.

In a large dictionary, such as the Oxford English Dictionary (O.E.D.), they form less than 1% of the language, but in a passage of everyday prose, they are about 25%.

Next are the Latin-based words. These came into English by way of France as a result of the Norman Conquest in 1066. Over ten thousand words were then added to the language.

At this point the language moved from Old English, the language of Beowulf, into Middle English, the language of Chaucer. Latin-based words are long words, usually with a prefix, a root and a suffix. Long vowels are represented in open syllables and silent-e syllables, rather than in vowel teams. Latin words are relatively easy to spell. Latin-based words form about 55%, or more than half our language.

Finally, there are Greek words. Greek is the language of science. Greek came into English at different times and in various ways, but it has become the language of science and medicine. Greek words are composed of two elements, usually nouns, and often connected by the letter o. They are easy to spell, once you have mastered a few consonant spellings. Greek forms about 11% of English words.

Well, you and your student may conclude, this does not seem to add up to 100%, and of course it doesn't. The answer to your query is that many English words are of unknown origin, or come from other languages. Some of this is because of the spread of the British Empire, on which once the sun never set. From India came words such as rajah, bungalow, sari, verandah, bangle, cheetah, chutney, and pajama. From Australia came kangaroo, koala, boomerang, and dingo. From Africa we got banjo, zebra, chimpanzee, tsetse, and safari. Finally in recent years, there has been an influx of Spanish words so that now everyone knows the meaning of nada, adios, casa, and vamos. Of course, words like tomato, potato, avocado, cocoa, chocolate, chili, condor, llama, tobacco, coyote, and armada have

Never Too Late. Diana Hanbury King. WVCED.com.

been in the language for much longer.

Given these statistics, in teaching you, would it make sense to focus on just the Anglo-Saxon part of the language? Of course not. That is why, even as we work to fill any gaps we find in your knowledge of basic Anglo-Saxon words, we are going to begin working with the more advanced Latin and Greek elements.

Importantly, in working with adults, you will be guided by their needs and interests, rather than by some fixed lesson plan of your own. The amount of time you devote to each activity will vary widely. At first you may spend most of the time working with open and closed syllables or practicing letter formations. Later, you might read for a whole hour, or devote an entire lesson to helping your student develop an expanded paragraph. The teaching you do will be very much diagnostic/prescriptive. You cannot afford to waste time teaching things he already knows. If your teaching results in frustration or boredom, you will lose him. He will begin skipping sessions and finally stop coming altogether. And that will probably be your fault.

I would like you to know that in the course of a lifetime of teaching, I have worked with a number of students who were non-readers, not at age nine or ten, but at twelve, fifteen, or even nineteen or twenty with barely first grade skills. I will tell you about just two of them.

Jason was the head of maintenance at a private school. His son was twelve and enrolled in a nearby public school. In an interview with the school superintendent, his dad was told, "Your son will never learn to read, but don't worry. There are plenty of job opportunities for bright dyslexics." Fortunately, his father ignored the advice and enrolled him in The Kildonan School, where he learned to read and write and went on to college.
Then one day I got a phone call from his mother, who told me he was at Dartmouth, finishing a doctorate degree.

9

Never Too Late. Diana Hanbury King. WVCED.com.

Then there was Wayne Lamade, to whom this book is dedicated. Wayne was twenty. He had suffered a detached retina, the result of a work-related accident, and had to keep one eye patched for years. His reading and writing were barely at a first-grade level. I was nervous as I had not worked with adults before. I said to him, "What if we spend all this time and you work really hard, and in the end you still cannot learn to read?" He answered, "Well, we'll never know if we don't try, will we?" So, I started teaching him, and literacy transformed his life. He ran a very successful trucking company and ended up at one point as president of the Indiana branch of the International Dyslexia Association.

In the course of this book, I have provided a sufficient number of examples of each activity to get you started; however, you will need to acquire the resources listed in the Appendix as you need them. Also, you would do well to read through this entire text before you begin your teaching. You will not be following the book sequentially, but carefully selecting the parts that are relevant to your student's needs. Some of what you do every day will depend on her mood. Does she seem tired, upset or discouraged? If so this might not be the moment to teach the new concept that you had planned for. You might be better off reading to her, having her read aloud, or suggesting that she might like to dictate some sentences, or even a paragraph to you. You might engage in list making, perhaps taking turns in coming up with items. You might have fun introducing a couple of Greek or Latin elements, or an interesting etymology. Several chapters of this book provide possibilities for exploring and discussing different aspects of our language.

Do make sure that your student experiences success in every lesson. If she does so, she will be motivated to keep coming to you for help.

Diana Hanbury King, Fall 2016

10

Never Too Late. Diana Hanbury King. WVCED.com.

Letter Sounds 1

"You don't understand. This is the first time in my life that I have ever read words." Jose, age 30.

Most adults, even those who cannot read, know the sounds of the consonants. This is because the name of the letter usually contains the sound, either followed by long e as in the following:

    bee, cee, dee, gee, pee, tee, vee, zee
or preceded by short e, as in the following:

    ef, el, em, en, es, ex

Two letters are the letter sound followed by long a: jay, kay

The remaining five are more problematic. To make the /h/, tell your student to pant like a dog, and to make the /r/ he should growl. The letter q begins like its name, but then adds a long u sound. Do not be surprised to find a student who thinks that the sound of w is /d/ and the sound of y is /w/! (Think about how we pronounce these letters to realize why.)

When we are working with young children, we usually begin with short vowels and three letter words, as these are more common, but when we teach adults, it makes better sense to start with long vowels and open and silent-e syllables.

Never Too Late. Diana Hanbury King. WVCED.com.

Since the sound of the long vowel is simply its name, this is a good starting point. Note that the sound for long y as a vowel is the same as long i.

Begin by reading some short words that are open syllables, such as…

go   no   so   hi   he   she   we   by   my   dry   cry   pry
fly   try   spy

Next, introduce the silent-e principle. Explain that the e is silent and that the vowel preceding it will say its name. If he hesitates, you might ask, "What is the name of that vowel?"

SILENT-E PRINCIPLE					
a-e	e-e	i-e	o-e	u-e	y-e
safe	eve	five	home	mule	type
late	eke	fine	hope	mute	style
fame		mile	rope	fuse	
gate		live	dome	cube	
game		hive	woke	June	
lake		like	joke	duke	
		pipe	smoke		

There are very few short e-e words because the long e sound is usually spelled ea or ee, and the Greek y-e occurs in only two common short words. The long u sound is often pronounced long /oo/, as in rule or rude—if the long u is too difficult to say as it is in flute, just try the /oo/ sound.

Many years ago, when I was teaching reading in a prison, I decided that my first lesson had to be a success, and I planned to introduce the silent-e principle. As we practiced these words, one of the inmates became visibly agitated and his voice higher in pitch. I said, "Jose, this is great. Relax, you are doing just fine."

Never Too Late. Diana Hanbury King. WVCED.com.

Jose slammed his fist on the table, raised his voice and almost shouted, "YOU don't understand. NONE OF YOU understand. NOBODY understands." I waited nervously. This was after all a maximum-security prison, and none of them were here for parking tickets. Then Jose continued, "This is the first time in my life that I have ever read words." And Jose was about thirty years old.

On another occasion, some years later, I was teaching a truck driver, a man in his mid thirties. After the second lesson, he came back in great excitement that he had been able to read the word "kitchen closed" on a door. He was thrilled.

Now in either case, had I started in the traditional way, as we would with a young child, by bringing out a deck of cards and teaching the first group of consonants and short a, the student would not have experienced this kind of immediate success.

Never Too Late. Diana Hanbury King. WVCED.com.

Flip Cards

"Chase had an incredibly difficult time at public school. The daily panic attacks were so severe that he could not talk, walk, or function for hours after. We tried everything under the planet to help him—tons of doctors, meetings, and even medication. Nothing helped. It only got worse. We found out that the treatment was really simple. The treatment was educational. And we never truly understood that until he came to Kildonan."   *A letter from Chase's parents*

Some teachers working with older students advocate using "nonsense words." I do not, as it is far more rewarding and empowering to be reading real words.

To create a deck of flip cards, using a marker or flair pen, write the first syllable on one side of the card, turn the card upside down and write the second syllable on the other side. Clip a corner off each card, so that you can keep the deck in order. Your student will read the first side; then, after you flip the card, he will read the second side, and finally pronounce the whole word. All the words in this deck are composed of open and silent-e syllables.

front   de

flip card example

back   ǝʇom

FLIP CARD EXAMPLES

ho bo	de ride	po lo	u nite
lo go	de fuse	pro vide	re volve
re late	re fuse	ha lo	e volve
re fine	di lute	de mote	e mote
re make	hu mane	de vote	re mote
be have	pro fane	de fine	si lo
re pute	po lite	so lo	de rive
pre game	lo co	tu na	de prive
he ro	po go	ve to	re late
e voke	pro mote	ze ro	

Many of the words your student has just read begin with Latin prefixes. This is probably a good time to introduce Latin elements. Explain that a prefix comes at the beginning of the word and that it changes the meaning. Your student will be familiar with the difference between happy and unhappy, lucky or unlucky, fortunate or unfortunate, as well as understand versus misunderstand, and behave versus misbehave.

You can begin with the prefixes that are open syllables. For now, this will be an oral exercise in which you talk and ask questions. You will not at this point expect him to read the words.

You: The prefix pre means before, as in pretest. Can you think of a word that means before school?"

Student: Preschool?

You: Right. How about a word that means to stop something before it happens?

Student: Prevent?

You: Yes. Can you think of a word that means to judge something before you know much about it?

Student: Prejudge?

You: Good. And, by the way, that is where the word prejudice comes from.

Never Too Late. Diana Hanbury King. WVCED.com.

You will point out to your student that Latin goes backwards. For instance, prejudge means "judge before," not "before judge." Introduce other words selected from this list in the same way:

pre- means before:
prehistory, prekindergarten, preview, preselect, prearrange, predawn, pretrial, predict, prewar, pre-op, prepare, preclude, prelude, premonition, predict, preamble, precaution, preset, preoccupied, precocious, preparatory, predecessor

The next day, in much the same way, you can introduce another prefix that is an open syllable.

re- means again:
reread, recopy, rearrange, reorganize, rewrite, review, redo, regroup, reposition, readjust, revote, reassemble, remarry, renew, reteach, reintroduce

It also has the meaning of **back**, as in reverse, return, refute, respond, response, regurgitate, recall, revoke, reset.

A third prefix that is an open syllable is **pro-**, with the meaning **for or forth:** pro-American, proceed, prochoice, pro-British, promote, protest, project.

Finally, you can teach **se-**, meaning **apart** as in seclude, but the problem with this one is that the e does not always retain the long sound. Examples include seduce, separate, segregate, select, secede, secret, and sequester.

Spend plenty of time talking about these words, as they may not all be familiar. You will be building vocabulary in the best possible way. If you are sufficiently clever in engaging him in the dialogue, the meaning of the prefix will stick in your student's mind. Of course, you can make drill cards

Never Too Late. Diana Hanbury King. WVCED.com.

with the root on one side and a key word and the meaning on the back side. Spaced review is also useful. Before he leaves the lesson, you can ask him, "So, what was our new prefix today?" And, at the beginning of the next lesson, you might ask, "Do you remember what pre- means?" And, if he has forgotten, you would provide a hint that would elicit the correct response.

Never Too Late. Diana Hanbury King. WVCED.com.

Introducing Short Vowels &
The Closed Syllable 3

"I have a paperback library of all the books I have read. I even stole books from school; if I read it, it went to Charlotte. I love short stories, about 25 pages. I read it, get it, and go on to the next story." Joe

So far you have taught your student two kinds of syllables, open and silent-e, both with long vowel sounds. While continuing to practice these, you will begin to prepare your student for the third syllable type, the closed syllable. The vowel in a closed syllable is short.

Short vowels are best introduced in a multisensory fashion, using both a specific key word and a hand signal that reflects the shape of the letter. It is crucial that the key word start with a short vowel that can be readily isolated. Do not use other key words, such as egg, Eskimo, Indian, or octopus. Before you attempt to read short-vowel words, you will practice this daily, even as you continue work with the long vowels.

A   Form your index finger and thumb into a semi-circle, as if holding an apple that you are ready to bite into. Say "a a-pple /a/" as you open your mouth wide.

E   Point your index finger down and make an e and continue in a circular, swirling motion, imitating an eddy (the motion of water running down a drain, or wind swirling leaves on the ground). As you do so, say "e

Never Too Late. Diana Hanbury King. WVCED.com.

eddy /e/." Your lips will be relatively relaxed, in order for the sound not to be confused with /i/.

I   Hold your index finger up and rub it on the back of your other hand. As you do so, say, "i -tchy /i/." As you pronounce this sound, your lips will be fairly tight, as in a smile. Pretend the dot on the i is the mosquito that just bit you.

O   With thumb and index finger, make a small circle in the shape of an olive. As you do so, say "o o-live /o/." Americans tend to make the o sound without rounding their lips so that it sounds more like /u/. You can alleviate this confusion by encouraging your student to round his lips.

U   Cup your thumb and index finger in the shape of the letter U and move your hand upward. As you do so, say "u u-pper /u/." Keep the vowel sound isolated—you do not want the word "up."

Once these sounds have been mastered, your student is ready to read closed syllables. You can explain the distinction between open and closed syllables by pronouncing pairs of words, such as hi/him, me/met, no/not, go/got, and fro/frog, and noticing that an open syllable ends with the lips slightly parted whereas in a closed syllable the lips are closed.

If you were working with a child, you would be starting with short three-letter words. Some teachers recommend using "nonsense syllables," but as I have already explained, I do not. A far more meaningful and useful activity is to continue working with flip cards, but this time include all three syllable types: open, closed, and silent e. A useful mnemonic is…

NO   open sylllable
NOT   closed syllable
NOTE   silent-e syllable

19

Never Too Late. Diana Hanbury King. WVCED.com.

MORE FLIP CARD EXAMPLES

ho tel	mo tel	o zone	gob lin
re lax	com pete	ben zene	hu mid
sol id	com pel	ra don	in vest
hab it	con fine	pep tone	in vite
gob lin	in hale	re pent	kid nap
Da vid	ex hale	lin den	pro vide
ban dit	ex it	en dure	pun ish
in dex	im bibe	cob web	pub lish
man date	in vite	cred it	sha ving
cap sule	mun dane	ba sin	un safe
con sole	um pire	div ide	re pel
dis pute	stam pede	e rupt	con text
in sane	im mune	cab in	di lute
en tire	de fine	van ish	e ven
es cape	re fine	ex pire	in vent
in vade	in vade	ex plode	ex pel
re late	o mit	gob let	dis pel

If your student makes a mistake, often a reminder or a question as to the type of syllable will suffice to enable her to provide the correct response. As you teach adults, you will probably find that they have acquired a sight vocabulary of some of the more common words. Also, when teaching children, we usually spend time working with blends, but most adults do not have difficulty in simply pronouncing one consonant after another. Blends have been included in some of the lists above, and in the phrases at the end of the next chapter on handwriting there are some common short sight words, as well as words that include sounds not yet taught.

Now that your student has learned closed syllables, you can go on to introduce several more Latin prefixes. Follow the same procedures as you did in introducing the first set of prefixes. The first prefix you introduce from this new group, ex-, begins over a thousand words. Start with the

Never Too Late. Diana Hanbury King. WVCED.com.

shorter, more common ones, and then introduce the longer and less familiar ones from time to time.

ex- means out as in exit.
extinct, exterior, ex-president, expose, expand, exhale, export, explore, expanse, extract, exceed, extinguish, exhibit, exile, exploit, exclude, execute, excavate, exempt, explode, exaggerate, excavate, exclusive, exterminate, exhaust, excommunicate, exonerate, exoskeleton, exorbitant, exception, exorcise, excursion, excrement, excruciating, exasperate

In talking about the more difficult words, you may want to explain how the prefix relates to the meaning. For instance, when we are exasperated, we often breathe out sharply, exorbitant expense is "out of orbit," and crabs and turtles have their skeletons outside of their bodies, hence exoskeletons. (We humans have endoskeletons, bones inside our bodies.)

Sometimes the letter x is dropped, and just the e- remains.
evict, evacuate, erode, elect, emit, eject, edit, emote, eradicate, evoke, elicit, eliminate,

sub- means under as in submarine.
subway, subject, subterfuge, substandard, subterranean, subsist, submit, subnormal, subzero, subtropical, submerge

in- or im- means not as in insane or impossible (or into as in invade, imbibe).
inaccurate, inefficient, insufficient, impasse, imperil, impute, improbable, immeasurable, inexcusable, inappropriate, impersonal, immoral, impious, immeasurable, imperfect, ingrown, inactive, incomplete, inanimate, inaudible, inconspicuous, incapacity, incautious, indigestible, indiscreet, indestructible, indefatigable, inexcusable, injustice, innumerable, insignificant, insensitive, insufferable, involuntary, independent, indefensible, infuse, invest, inbreed, income, indent, induct, incision,

Never Too Late. Diana Hanbury King. WVCED.com.

inflate, infiltrate, inbound, inhale, include, immerse, implode, import, imprison, immigrate, imprint, impress, implant, impetus

con- or com- means with or together, as in combine.
connect, contain, congress, convene, compel, combat, command, context, consensus, confluence, congregation, compact, complement, convoke, convocation, confusion

ab- means away from, as in absent and ad- means to or towards, as in advance. You can avoid confusion by pointing out that in ab- the b turns away from the a, and in ad- it turns towards the a.

abscond, abolish, abundant, abnormal, abstain, abstention, abduct, abstract, abort

advent, addict, adjust, admit, administer, adopt, adapt, adjacent, adverb, adjective, adjunct, advocate, admit, adverse

trans- means across as in transport.
trans-Atlantic, transform, transmit, transmission, trans-Pacific, transfer, translate, transcontinental, transparent

post- means after as in postpone.
postwar, postelection, postpartum, postmortem, posthumous
Incidentally, p.m. is an abbreviation for post-meridian, and a.m. for ante-meridian, meaning after or before the sun reaches the highest point in the sky.

dis- means not, as in dislike, or apart as in dislocate.
disagree, disagreeable, dispose, disappear, disarray, dispute, disheveled, disorganized, disarrange, disapprove, discontent, disbelieve, discourteous, disorderly, distrust, disrespect, disperse, dispatch, dismiss, disown, disqualify, discharge, dissipate, dismember, disillusion, disintegrate,

Never Too Late. Diana Hanbury King. WVCED.com.

disentangle

Here again, as was the case with ex-, sometimes the final letter is omitted, and the prefix becomes di-.

divide, divorce, dilate, digress, digest, diverse

You can now also introduce for reading two useful Latin syllables that occur at the ends of words. If you divide these words into syllables, your student will succeed even with the three- syllable sequences.

-tion is pronounced /shun/.

-TION = /SHUN/ EXAMPLES		
men tion	am bi tion (i is short	in ven tion
mo tion	before -tion)	cel e bra tion
lo tion	va ca tion	de struc tion
no tion	ac tion	in ten tion
func tion	con nec tion	re ac tion
na tion	pro tec tion	dis trac tion
sta tion	e lec tion	con fron ta tion
so lu tion	in vo ca tion	
do na tion	col lec tion	

-sion pronounced /zhun/.
e ro sion   in va sion   ex plo sion   vision (i is short)

The i preceding the -sion or -tion (as above in am bi tion and vi sion) is often short.
di vi sion   de ci sion   e li sion

When the –sion is preceded by s, n, or l (as in *Saturday Night Live*, or the word snail) it will usually be pronounced /shun/.

ex ten sion   ap pre hen sion   per mis sion   dis cuss ion
pro pul sion   re vul sion   re mis sion

Never Too Late. Diana Hanbury King. WVCED.com.

Sometimes you have to try both pronunciations and pick the one that sounds right.

You will notice one more thing that is a great help in decoding Latin-based words. In these words the vowel immediately before the /sh/ or /zh/ sound follows the following rule: a, o, and u will be long, i is always short, and e may vary. Note the following carefully:

invitation	invasion	motion	division	ammunition
erosion	execution	illusion	lesion	profession
session				

This principle applies to vowels immediately preceding the ci or ti spelling of the /sh/ sound.
vicious, spacious, precious and special (but specious)

Knowing this principle will enable the decoding of dozens of words and is worth spending time addressing.

Never Too Late. Diana Hanbury King. WVCED.com.

"I can count the people I've told I'm dyslexic on one hand. In general, no. I don't. That's just something I don't. The few relationships I've had, I have told them. But no, I generally don't broadcast it at all. but dyslexia is always in the back of my mind, you know."   Ed

At the clinic for adolescents in Boston, teen-agers came in with various inexplicable physical symptoms. Finally, according to my mentor, Helene Durbrow, it was decided to make a test of reading and writing skills part of the intake routine. And the cause of the problems became clear.

Begin to introduce the pairs of consonants, which your student may already know. They are called digraphs, a word that means two letters. Start with sh as in ship and ch as in chin, and then add th as in this or thin and the Greek ph as in phone.

Read a few one-syllable words before making flip cards to add to the pack.

sh	shine	shape	fish	rash	hush	gosh	trash	shun
ash	hash	dish	posh	shame	shin	mash	rush	shift
shut	ship							

ch	chop	rich	such	much	chap	chip	chest	chum
ranch	pinch	inch	bunch	lunch	hunch	chin		

25

Never Too Late. Diana Hanbury King. WVCED.com.

th	that	thin	these	those	theme	with	pith	fifth
photo	phone	graph	Ralph	Phil	this	Philadelphia		

While you are at it, you might as well add ck:

ck	sick	sack	sock	tick	tack	clock	shock	trick
slick								

Now your student can read words such as...

pho to   ship shape   sun shade   rel ish   back track
ath lete   sun shine   Phil lip   re shape   pho no graph
pho to graph   tel e graph

At this point you may want to introduce the fact that three of the consonants have two sounds—something you may have already noticed in the lists.

S often sounds like /z/ and is actually the most common way of spelling the /z/ sound.

It is /z/ when it comes between two vowels.
rose   rise   these   those   hose   nose   pose

And at the end of words.
is   his   hums   dogs   digs   rags   rubs   runs   sums
ribs   was

If the /s/ sound does not sound right, try the /z/ sound. Incidentally, this is often a problem for those for whom English is not their first language as they continue to use only /s/ for the letter.

C and G behave in the same way: each has two pronunciations.

C says /k / as in cat and /s/ before e, i, and y as in cent, city, and fancy.

Never Too Late. Diana Hanbury King. WVCED.com.

G says /g/ as in go and /j/ before e, i, and y as in gentle, ginger, and gym.

This principle takes much practice because it involves looking ahead to the next letter before deciding on the c or g sound.

You might want to make a pack of cards or a list containing the following: ce, ci, cl, cr, cy, ge, gi, gl, gr, gy. Shuffle them and practice having your student give just the sound of the first letter. In the case of g there are some exceptions, including get, give, girl, gift, tiger.

A useful "r-controlled" sound is /er/ as in her.

MORE FLIP CARD EXAMPLES				
pre fer	of fer	sum mer	yon der	po ker
hun ter	hec tic	fish er	rub ber	ten der
suf fer	pen cil	per fect	tem per	con cert
num ber	re cess	Fran cis	cin der	gin ger
her mit	me ter	Her bert	ci der	su per
ba ker	Pe ter	zip per	gro cer	re cent
mem ber	pan ther	traf fic	de cide	pre cede
shel ter	di ner	riv er	re cite	re cede
blis ter	dri ver	of fer	de cent	con cede
mon ster	win ter	up per	so ber	

With the above in mind, you can add many words to the pack of flip cards. You might at this point teach more about the letter y. You have already taught the consonant sound, as in yes, and the long vowel sound, as in my. Y at the end of multi-syllabic words is often pronounced as long e.

• • •

Never Too Late. Diana Hanbury King. WVCED.com.

MORE FLIP CARD EXAMPLES
(Y AT END OF MULTI-SYLLABIC WORDS)

hap py	brave ly	sun ny	Ran dy	crus ty
luck y	sim ply	rain y	safe ly	lus ty
fun ny	cra zy	Sal ly	safe ty	rus ty
sil ly	ha zy	Jim my	san dy	mis ty
odd ly	la zy	Pol ly	win dy	fog gy
pluck y	fuz zy	han dy	mud dy	dad dy

Never Too Late. Diana Hanbury King. WVCED.com.

Handwriting: The Move to Cursive 5

Karl Kline, an eminent Vancouver psychiatrist, once told me, "I often find that if I can place a child with the right tutor, there is no need for the psychotherapy."

In all likelihood, the adult with whom you are working will be writing in a mixture of upper and lower case print, with many of the letters incorrectly formed. While you may want to take the time to correct the malformations, your best bet is to begin work on cursive right from the start. Cursive has several advantages. There are fewer reversible letters. Writing the word as a unit facilitates spelling. It is undeniably much faster. Recent research has found many other benefits. Finally, for your student, it can be a proud achievement. Work on handwriting every day while you are working with the first three syllable types.

If your student is already familiar with the lower-case print formations, the transition to cursive will be facilitated. The following letters are the same as print formations, except that they begin on the line and end with a serif:
a, d, e, i, m, n, p, t, u, x

And the following substitute a loop for the straight line:
g, h, j, l, q, y, and even z

With cursive g and j, we head left to finish the loop. With f and q, we head right to finish the bottom loop:
quest, queen, quit versus for, off, fist

You can demonstrate the similarity between print and cursive to your student by superimposing the cursive form over the printed letter.

Teach the letters a few at a time, beginning with the easier formations. Note that all letters begin on the line and all end with a serif, or little smile, that facilitates the connection to the next letter.

Stress the fact that "We never lift up." Finish writing the word, and then go back for the four "finish-later letters," which are i, j, t, and x.

The next group is sometimes called the "two-o'clock letters" because they are formed by starting on the line and circling up around the clock to two o'clock. This group includes c, a, d, g, and q. Since q is always followed by u, you may as well introduce it here. In writing d, note that you make the a but go on up and then backtrack down to finish with a serif. You can now begin to practice writing a wide selection of words.

cat	can	call	cent	act	am	an	ant	and
man	mall	meat	eat	mean	den	dam	din	dim
dent	land	dell	dill	add	dust	dime	get	gland
age	cage	edge	ledge	mug	gun	gin	quit	queen
quince	quintet	dune	dunce	ridge	rigid	rancid		

If you have not already thought to do so, now might be the moment to have your student practice writing his name in cursive. No need to worry about cursive capitals—he can use the print formations, as do many adults.

Note that "g and j go the same way."
just jump jog jest joke jam jail

Never Too Late. Diana Hanbury King. WVCED.com.

The four "bridge letters" are relatively easy to form. The problem arises in joining them with the next letters. The best way to practice this is to join them with just a single letter. Especially tricky are the connections to m, n, r, and s, as so much of the letter seems to be missing.

Every day, begin by having your student write the alphabet in two lines, a to m and n to z. Then spend a little time working on any problem letters.

Do not worry if at first the writing is very slow. Speed will come in due course with practice. You cannot hurry the beginning stages.

Next, begin copying short phrases rather than just single words. Copy each just twice. Again, this is meant as a handwriting exercise, and you can read each phrase to your student before she copies it.

PHRASES FOR COPYING

into the city	by myself	grab a bite	win a prize
for the kids	sit on a bench	had a fit	walk all day
hoping for rain	fun and games	bit the dust	came in late
go to bed	a picnic lunch	ran the game	in the shade
a safe place	lost the keys	stop at the gate	went to war
at the game	drove home	by my side	ran from home
a bad test	spent the cash	take the best	into the deep
came to rest	came late	woke the kid	high in the sky
left home	got the joke	spoke to him	fell from a tree
went for a run	sit in the sun	came in last	quit the job

Never Too Late. Diana Hanbury King. WVCED.com.

The Vowel Teams 6

"At Chico State…I went to one or two tutoring sessions but never went back. Their approach was that it was okay not to read everything, and their way of going through a text was to blank out certain words and make sure you comprehended everything regardless of whether you read the words or not. I didn't feel that was a proper approach." Melissa

There are about forty vowel teams, and they occur in words of Anglo-Saxon origin. Unfortunately, they form the common words, which children often encounter first. Your adult student might be familiar with many of these words and may even have figured out the sounds. You may find you can introduce the more common ones fairly quickly.

Use the key words suggested for each, and perhaps make pictures to illustrate them. Then teach each of these pairs as a team, rather than saying that the first vowel is long and the second is silent. Avoid saying, "When two vowels go walking, the first does the talking," because you will be wrong about half the time!

A good place to begin is with the vowel teams that make a long vowel sound. Here they are in order with the key words:

ai and ay   sail away

ee and ea   see the sea

igh and y	night sky
oa and ow	boat is slow
ue and ew	rescue a few

You can make it into a little story. We sail away and see the sea and the night sky. Our boat is slow, but we rescue a few.

You can begin reading them in lists containing just one sound, and then mix them up. (See the Appendix for good resources.)

Then move on to three combinations that make a different sound.

oo has two sounds, as in moon and book.   Food is good.

oi and oy have the same sound   Oil the toy.

au and aw are less common.   August was awful.

The combination ea has three possible sounds.   Eat bread with steak.

The long e sound is the most common, but there are about 40 words where it has a short e sound. Here are a few of the most frequent ones.

head	dead	bread	breath	death	deaf	thread
wealth	meant	health	weather	sweat	sweater	spread
dread	stealth	weapon				

In three common words it sounds like long a: great, break, steak, and you could include yea.

33

Never Too Late. Diana Hanbury King. WVCED.com.

As you read with your student, you will come across various oddities, mostly in these short Anglo-Saxon words. These may include silent letters such as the k in knee, the g in gnome, and the w in write. Sometimes, vowels behave in unexpected ways, as does a before l as in all and walk, or the o in one or once. You can explain that silent letters used to be pronounced (In fact, German still pronounces the k and g before n.) and that spelling has not always kept up with changes in pronunciation. Deal with these matters on a "need-to-know" basis. Never forget, English is still a fundamentally phonetic language.

Never Too Late. Diana Hanbury King. WVCED.com.

Oral Reading

"When I was in school I couldn't read Curious George, but now I can."
Inmate at Fallsburg prison.

When I was teaching reading to inmates in a prison, one day I wandered into the library. After looking around, I asked the librarian why there did not appear to be a section of easier reading books. He said, "None of the men would ever check them out!"

I consulted with my friend and colleague, Polly Ash, and we acquired some children's books. In no time at all, the librarian could not keep on the shelf enough copies of the Wayside Schoolhouse series, and we had to bring in more. Later, an inmate remarked to me, "When I was in school I couldn't read Curious George, but now I can." Reading with my group in the same prison, we finished several of the easy beginner books and then worked our way up to E.B. White's *Charlotte's Web*, a story they adored. When we came to the chapter where Wilbur tries to escape, they laughed so hard I thought they might fall off their chairs.

Many years later, I spent some time in China working with a group of teachers. My colleagues offered me a choice, and I said I would like to work with the ones who were the weakest in English, and I was given a class of seventeen. They were supposed to be teaching English to children in nearby schools, and while they had all graduated from college, their English pronunciation was surprisingly deficient. I know no Chinese,

Never Too Late. Diana Hanbury King. WVCED.com.

but was given an aide to interpret for me when my students had questions or did not understand my directions. Fortunately, I had a room with an overhead projector, and I was able to put the books I had brought on the screen. I had a good supply of the Little Bear series, the Frog and Toad books and even the Nutshell Library. Later, we went on to read *My Father's Dragon* and Mark Twain's "War Prayer"—the latter was their favorite. Sometimes the group read chorally, and sometimes individuals took roles.

Even in a group of that size, I could immediately hear if even one person was mispronouncing a word, and I would model the sentence before asking the class to try again. Incidentally, this might be a good procedure for classroom teachers to follow, since no child is singled out, and if he cannot read a word he can just listen, rather than be embarrassed.

Most of the strictly phonetically based books are boring and use stilted language in an effort to avoid irregular words. I have found that adults can certainly enjoy the Lobel books or any others in the beginning reader series. Other possibilities are *Stone Fox* and even Hemingway's *The Old Man and the Sea*.

Sometimes it is fun for a change to read short poetry. I have had success with some of Robert Frost, Emily Dickinson, Edna St. Vincent Millay, and Langston Hughes. Another possibility is to choose a proverb, read it, and discuss its meaning. The interesting thing about proverbs is that they are a form of metaphor. For instance, "Don't count your chickens before they hatch" is not about chickens, nor is "Too many cooks spoil the broth" about cooking.

Margaret Rawson once told me that students should be reading from real books, even if they could read only a few words on each page, with the teacher doing the rest of the reading. It is easy to pick a book and say from time to time, "Here's a word you can read!"

I tend to sit catty-corner from my student and to use a pencil to keep the place. Some people advocate sitting opposite, or even having two books, but I find this more comfortable. I can simply stop the pencil if the student misreads or omits a word, and this silent signal is enough to let him know to take another look. I can also use my pencil to divide a word into syllables. If a student cannot read a word, a simple reminder as to the sound is usually enough.

I once watched a teacher working with a group of fourth graders. A child was stuck on the word thirsty. The teacher said, "Imagine it is a very hot day. You have been playing outside in the sun and you cannot wait to go back into the house where you know your mom will give you a drink of cold lemonade. You are feeling very_____." And the child said, "Thirsty."

Well, in her place, I would have simply said, "ir says /er/. Now you can read the word." And I would have made a note to review that sound and to practice words like girl, shirt, skirt, dirt and first. Too often teachers encourage students to "Look at the pictures," or "Try the sentence again and put in a word that makes sense." Students trained in this manner go back to the beginning of the sentence the minute they see a long word or a word they think they cannot decode. Of course, if the word is one a student cannot decode, the teacher should simply supply it. Once I watched a teacher telling a boy stuck on the word geography to "just sound it out!" The child did so, all eight sounds. Then the teacher said, "Now put the sounds together." And, not surprisingly, he couldn't.

Often, nothing is needed other than waiting silently for the student to remember a sound combination and to put the word together. The process should not be hurried. You can say, "I think you can read it," or "Take your time." Above all, allow your student time to think and to process, and avoid any body language that signals impatience – let alone exasperation. Remember, just because she knew it yesterday does not mean that she will remember it today. Proper names are particularly difficult, and you

Never Too Late. Diana Hanbury King. WVCED.com.

may reach the end of a book before your student can unerringly pronounce the names of the main characters – meanwhile, you should simply supply them.

Never Too Late. Diana Hanbury King. WVCED.com.

Listening to Books 8

"Without the experience of being read to, I never would have made the effort to learn to read myself." Inmate

The other day I heard a story that I would like to share. A friend of mine told me about her son. His story was heart-breaking. His life had not turned out well, and he ended up dying in prison. But before he died, he was in the habit of reading aloud to his fellow inmates, many of whom were illiterate. One book he read to them was *Me and Marley*, the story of a man and his dog. When they reached the ending, many of the men were so moved that they had to disguise their tears by pretending they had allergies. After the death of my friend's son, one of the inmates went on to learn to read, but he said that without the experience of being read to, he never would have made the effort.

Many of the children you teach have parents who have read to them regularly, often at bedtime. The adults with whom you work may not have had this experience. Listening to a recorded book, by the way, is not the same as having someone read it to you and discuss it with you.

So, I would suggest that you spend time reading aloud to your student. Choose the book carefully, based on his knowledge, his interests, and his level of sophistication. It might be a Beatrix Potter Book, a Roald Dahl, *The Wind in the Willows*, *Charlotte's Web*, or perhaps a classic, such as

Never Too Late. Diana Hanbury King. WVCED.com.

Robinson Crusoe, *Heidi*, or even *Tom Sawyer*. Spend time talking about the book.

Reading aloud is one of the very best ways of developing comprehension and engaging your student in the reading. This will not happen if all he is doing is listening to a recording.

One day a fifteen-year-old, to my surprise and annoyance, arrived about ten minutes late for a tutoring session. I will never forget his explanation. He had just finished a book—it might have been *The Pearl*, or *Of Mice and Men*, I am not sure which. He explained that the ending was so sad that he had to take time out before he could stop crying. Unlike students who have enjoyed literature and the emotions that come with it as we identify with the characters, this was nothing he had experienced before.

Syllabication

"The last year at public school, Chase missed more days due to school refusal than days he was there. And the days he was there were normally partial days as he either came in late or had to leave early due to the anxiety."   *Excerpted from a letter written by Chase's parents*

Until now you have been reading multisyllabic words on flip cards, one syllable at a time. Now you can begin to teach your student how to break up two-syllable words on her own.

There are three formulas for syllabication. Begin by having your student code the vowels and consonants, beginning with the first vowel. You can write v or c under each letter, or better yet, just put a dot under each vowel—maybe in color.

#1 When two consonants stand between two vowels, divide between the consonants. We call these RABBIT words.

muffin	gossip	happen	dentist
commit	butter	tennis	inmate
unless	hammer	goblin	combine
bandit	hamlet	dispute	submit
tonsil	index	costume	content

Never Too Late. Diana Hanbury King. WVCED.com.

IMPORTANT: Teach your student to divide by swooping under each syllable, rather than making a slash, which tends to look like another letter.

After a while, you can say to your student, "Just use your eyes."

When one consonant stands between two vowels, there is a choice of rules.

#2 Divide after the first vowel. You will have created an open syllable and the vowel will be long. We call these TI-GER words.

hotel	climax	silent	relate
spoken	relate	music	hotel
vacate	relax	ozone	moment

Always try this first because it is more common than #3.

#3 Divide after the consonant that follows the first vowel. You will have closed the syllable, and the vowel will be short. We call these CAM-EL words.

lemon	planet	habit	cabin
solid	banish	seven	copy
punish	limit	tepid	atom

Sometimes it is fun to play a game of reading the word both ways. For example, is it a ho tel or a hot el, a pla net or a plan et, a ca bin or a cab in.

If you treat blends, digraphs, and vowel teams like a single letter, there is no need to add more rules. Just circle the combination and follow the above three rules. Here are some for practice:

Never Too Late. Diana Hanbury King. WVCED.com.

re fresh ment	ship shape	main stream
ath lete	fish hook	dock side
mun ching	spoi ling	foo lish

English has many compound words. These words can be tackled by reading one word at a time and then putting the two together.

COMPOUND WORDS

snowman	sidewalk	fireplace	horseback	dockside
backpack	rainfall	mailman	boxcar	paintbrush
snowplow	suntan	doorstop	hoofpick	funfair
trapdoor	mousetrap	fishhook	ramrod	showboat
desktop	stepladder	teacup	teabag	doorstep
doorway	sunrise	sunset	starlight	peapod
moonlight	fistfight	snowstorm	shipshape	slipshod
inchworm	raindrop	snowdrop	mainstream	horseshoe

43

The Consonant-LE Syllable　10

"What I do now for a living is what they told me I would never be able to do." David, a technical manual writer

So far your student has been working with four kinds of syllables, the open closed, and silent-e, and the vowel team. Now you can introduce a fifth syllable, the consonant-le syllable. This syllable comes at the end of a word. Do not try to pronounce these syllables in isolation, as this is tricky because actually the letter l functions as the vowel. Just look at them and note that the consonant is followed by le.

-ble -dle -cle -fle -gle -kle -ple -tle -zle

The rule for dividing these words is CONSONANT-LE, COUNT BACK 3 or, if you prefer, CIRCLE 3.

CONSONANT-LE WORDS				
lit tle	daz zle	ti tle	ket tle	tri fle
ma ple	a ble	sta ble	wob ble	shut tle
ri fle	snug gle	ap ple	fiz zle	nim ble
rip ple	wrig gle	han dle	la dle	ram ble
mid dle	i dle	trem ble	bot tle	snif fle
sad dle	bum ble	ta ble	fid dle	fee ble
bri dle	drib ble	nee dle	stee ple	cir cle
Bi ble	ea gle	can dle	ruf fle	
hud dle	poo dle	bat tle	crum ble	

Never Too Late. Diana Hanbury King. WVCED.com.

Again, as soon as possible, tell your student, "Just use your eyes."

You will notice that in these words the t is silent:
castle, wrestle, hustle, bustle, rustle, thistle

And that in these words the division is between the c and the k:
crackle, freckle, tickle, chuckle, buckle

In both cases, the first syllable is closed and the vowel is short.

The R-Controlled Syllable   11

"I do feel the need for more schooling, but it is unfortunate that I don't like to read books—I hate reading. I only read magazines. My dad is dyslexic, and he's an avid reader. Mother's dyslexic. My brother is real dyslexic…. Mostly I read trade magazines, like Builder *and* Home Building*. As far as willpower goes, if I really want to do it, I'll do it. That has been a real asset."*   *Clem*

Now, your student can learn the last of the six syllable types. In this syllable, the r controls, or changes, the sound of the vowel. She has already learned one of them, the er with the /er/ sound.

She probably already knows the word car, and you can quickly add a selection of other ar words, such as…

far	farm	yard	hard	chart	barn	arm	par	partner
target	marsh	yarn	spark	shark	darn	garden	harvest	charm
dark	art	artist	carpet	march	carp	varnish	tarnish	sharper
carpenter		harness						

Next is or, as in the word for, which she may well know. She should have no problem with these:

storm	corn	horn	dorm	form	ford	porch	deplore	north
horse	fore	forget	hornet	forge	forth	gore	forgave	more
store	fork	adorn	forlorn	adore	restore	normal	morning	

Never Too Late. Diana Hanbury King. WVCED.com.

After w /er/ is spelled or in a few common words:

work   worm   worth   worry   worse   worst   worth   worthy

Finally, there are other ways to spell the /er/ sound. Any vowel followed by r can have the /er/ sound. Once your student knows this, she will have no trouble reading these words:

shirt	dirt	third	skirt	twirl	swirl	birth	birthday	girth
stir	chirp	birch	fir	squirt	hurt	burn	turn	purple
murder	survive	burst	lurk	church	turtle	Turkish	disturb	fur

At the end of long words or and ar also have the /er/sound:

words meaning people:

		doctor
major	minor	visitor
collector	inspector	professor
director	elector	confessor

words following l:

		solar
similar	regular	peculiar
dollar	collar	cellar
popular		

So, to sum up, any vowel followed by r can have the /er/ sound. This is not a problem for reading, but it is certainly one for spelling.

Finally, in a small group of common short words, the /er/ sound is spelled ear.

earl   early   pearl   search   earn   learn   earnest

Here is a sentence that contains all six /er/ spellings.
Her early bird hurt the worm in the cellar.

Never Too Late. Diana Hanbury King. WVCED.com.

"Dyslexia is an advantage when you are working with blueprints. You get your blueprint and most of the time you get one picture, and you have to turn it ninety or a hundred and eighty degrees and I find that very easy. Then blueprints are also always backwards in the printing , but when you do it on a part it's got to be forward—you have to turn it."   *Jeff*

Wait till your student has mastered handwriting—just lower-case is sufficient. He can continue to print capitals, or if he decides he wants to learn the cursive capital formations, you can acquire one of the workbooks listed in the resources section of the appendix.

You can dictate groups of words with silent-e syllables or with any one of the vowel teams—do not mix them up. Once you have dictated ten or fifteen of them, you can ask your student to select a few to use in a sentence.   You may have to remind him to begin with a capital and end with a period. If he asks for help with the spelling of a word, just supply it. If you ask him to "sound it out," or you say, "that is a word you know," you will interrupt his thinking process. Teach him to skip lines and use the wide lined rather than the college-ruled paper.

Gradually, encourage longer sentences by asking when, how, where, or why.

For instance, if he were to write "I went to the store," you could elicit a longer sentence by asking questions, so that the final result might be "This morning I quickly went to the store because we were out of milk." If he were to write, "The dog ran," you might elicit…" Just now, the brown dog ran across the road because it wanted to chase a cat."

NEVER correct his spelling by marking his paper, let alone in red! If he misspells a word you think he really needs to know, you can say, "This is a good word for you to learn, and I am going to add it to your personal spelling pack."

Some of your work with sentences should be done orally.

You can work with the different kinds of sentences: statements (the most common), questions, commands, and exclamations. Say a sentence and ask him which kind it is, or have him give examples of his own.

You can explain that a sentence always has two things:
The subject tells who or what the sentence is about.
The predicate tells something about the subject.

You can practice this with oral exercises in which you provide the

PERSONAL SPELLING PACKS

At first you will be selecting words from the student's mistakes in sentence, paragraph and essay writing. Write the word to be spelled on one side, if possible adding a mnemonic device, e.g. meet on the street, meat to eat, and group words with similar patterns on the same card, e.g. walk and talk, boat, float, and soap. Use a flair pen and write in cursive if your student uses cursive. Test the words weekly, and place a √ or an x each time beginning on the upper left -hand corner of the card. When the word has been spelled correctly, place a / and retire the card to "the graveyard". Organize the cards in categories, new and x, √, √√. Students practice writing them, never more than five times, and use each in a sentence. As the student learns more about sentence structure, you can ask for compound or complex sentences, or, at an advanced stage, even sentences in different tenses or using common or proper nouns, adjectives, or adverbs in order to make the task more varied and interesting. At a later stage, you could dictate words from a standard list.

Never Too Late. Diana Hanbury King. WVCED.com.

subject, and he contributes the predicate, or visa-versa. You will note that in command sentences, there is no stated subject, e.g., "Please close the window." In these sentences there is no need for the subject to be stated because it is always you.

In normal conversation, we may not always talk in complete sentences, but in writing, our sentences must be complete.

There are three types of sentences:

Simple sentence
A sentence with a subject and a predicate is a simple sentence, but notice that such a sentence can have a double subject, a double predicate, or even both.
Double subject: The boys and girls threw snowballs.
Double predicate: The boys threw snowballs and made a snowman.
Both: The boys and girls threw snowballs and made a snowman.

Compound sentence
A compound sentence, like a compound word, is two sentences put together, each of which can stand alone. For the moment, just work with *and* and *but*.

I would like to try that new restaurant, and we shall have dinner there tomorrow night.
I would like to try that new restaurant, but it is too expensive.

Sally wants to learn to swim, and her father is teaching her.
Sally wants to learn to swim, but she is afraid of the water.

The sun is shining, and the weather is warm.
The sun is shining, but there is an icy wind.

Never Too Late. Diana Hanbury King. WVCED.com.

You will notice that *and* signals an idea continuing in the same direction, and *but* signals a reversal from the expected. You can practice these orally by beginning a sentence and having your student finish it with *and* or *but*.

At a later date you can introduce the rest of these words. (Incidentally, they are called coordinating conjunctions.) Here is an example of each:

We can watch a movie, or Susan can take us to the concert.
She cannot sing, nor can she play the piano.
We must hurry, for night is falling.
Tom has difficulty with his algebra class, yet he aced yesterday's test.

In a compound sentence the comma is required. Notice that both parts (called clauses) can stand alone.

Refer to the appendix for more materials on this and other aspects of grammar.

Wait a while before you introduce the next kind of sentence.

Complex sentence or "flip sentence"
A complex sentence has two parts, one that can stand alone and one that cannot. The part that can stand alone is called the main or independent clause. The part that cannot is called the subordinate or dependent clause, and it begins with a subordinating conjunction. Having a list of these conjunctions handy would be useful for your student. Begin by having your student finish sentences orally. You will give the first part, and he will supply the end.

If it rains,   When she got home,
Although it is late,   Because you are under twenty-one,
Since Dad had to work late,   Unless it snows,
As my car is in the shop,

You could write down the endings he suggests, then talk about them, and finally show how they can be flipped, so that the main part comes at the beginning.

In the first of each pair, a comma is needed. In the second it is not.

Compare:

Because it is getting dark, we must hurry home.
We must hurry home because it is getting dark.

Although she never seems to study, she is getting good grades.
She is getting good grades although she never seems to study.

If the icecaps continue to melt, the sea level will rise.
The sea level will rise if the icecaps continue to melt.

When the music was over, the audience applauded.
The audience applauded when the music was over.

Unless it snows, we will not be sledding today.
We will not be sledding today unless it snows.

As my car is in the shop, I will have to take the bus to work.
I will have to take the bus to work as my car is in the shop.

If nobody answers your knock, you could ring the doorbell.
You could ring the doorbell if nobody answers your knock.

Before it starts to rain, we should bring in the laundry.
We should bring in the laundry before it starts to rain.

Never Too Late. Diana Hanbury King. WVCED.com.

More Latin 13

"I read magazines and theory books. I don't do as much reading as I should. Being dyslexic is not a hindrance to me in music, but it might be in the business end…you have to be on your toes and know how to manage money and conduct yourself. I feel from dyslexia I have the edge in going off using my ear and experimenting….. It's unique. It's what I am striving for. Maybe there is something magical about being dyslexic."   James

Your student will already have worked with some Latin prefixes and a couple of endings. Now you could begin to introduce some of the roots, which form the most important and interesting part of these long words. Latin roots are mostly verbs. Introduce them by engaging your student in a dialogue, such as the models that follow here.

You: If I have a portable computer, or a portable piece of baggage, what does that mean?

Student: Does it mean you can carry it? [If your student cannot come up with the meaning, you would simply say, "It means I can carry it. Port means carry."]

You: Yes, port means carry. Can you use a prefix you have learned that means to carry out of the country?

Student: Export?

You: Right. And how about a word that means to carry into a country?

Student: Import. But what about airport?

You: Yes. And a seaport or an airport is a place where they carry things

53

Never Too Late. Diana Hanbury King. WVCED.com.

in and out. And I guess a carport is a place to which you carry your car. Sometimes when you travel, you can get someone to carry your bags. What are people who do this called? Use your root.

Student: Porters?

You: Yes, although sometimes we call them "redcaps." Now people who make a lot of problems or engage in illegal activities might be forced to leave a country. They would be.......?

Student: Deported?

You: Yes. [If your student cannot think of the word, say, "Use the prefix de-."]

You: When you were in school, the teachers sent back to your home a card that had your grades on it.

Student: A report card!

You: Of course.

And perhaps the next day, you would introduce another root in much the same fashion.

You: I wear spectacles to help me see when I am reading. What do you think spect might mean?

Student: See?

You: Yes. And what do you call the people who come to watch a football game?

Student: Spectators.

You: Good. Now, how might you describe a really wonderful show of firework? Start with your root.

Student: Spectacular.

You: Good. You can form dozens of words with this root by adding prefixes and suffixes. For instance, inspect, respect, disrespect, prospect, spectacle, and circumspect.

You could talk about some of these other words in more detail. For instance, you might take the opportunity of introducing a new prefix,

54

Never Too Late. Diana Hanbury King. WVCED.com.

circum- meaning around. Your student might know that the circumference of a circle is the distance around it, and you could go on to explain that being circumspect means looking around you, or being cautious, and circumstances are the things that are around you, and even that Magellan was the first to circumnavigate the earth.

And a couple more roots:
You: Do you know what a rupture is?
Student: I guess it is some sort of a break.
You: Yes. And if a volcano erupts, what does it do?
Student: It breaks out.
You: And if you disrupt your classroom or disrupt a meeting, what do you do?
Student: I guess it means you kind of break things up.
You: Yes, and you might be called disruptive. Now if two people are talking, and you break into the conversation, what are you doing?
Student: Interrupting.
You: Yes, and what you do would be called an interruption. Inter is not a prefix we have studied. I wonder if you could guess its meaning if you think about what you do when you intercept a ball, or if there is an intermission in a play?
Student: Could it mean something that comes between?
You: Certainly. And another good word might be interfere.
Student: How about the word intercom?
You: Yes, indeed. It is actually an abbreviation for intercommunication, which means communicating between people.

And then ject:
You: A pilot in a plane might have an ejection button. When he pushes it, it throws him out of the plane so that he can parachute to safety. Ject means to throw. Can you use the prefix re- and make a word that means to throw back?
Student: Reject.

Never Too Late. Diana Hanbury King. WVCED.com.

You: Yes. And if a doctor gives you a shot, it would be called an…

Student: Injection.

You: Right. And there are lots of other ject words, such as object, subject, project, dejected, and so forth.

You: Maybe you know that some animals are carnivores, and others like cows are herbivores. Most people are omnivores. What do you think that means?

Student: I guess we eat everything.

You: Right. Omni means everything. Potent means powerful.

Can you use your root to make a word that means all-powerful?

Student: Omnipotent.

You: Good. Now there is another similar word that means all-knowing. Omniscient. Could you use omniscient in a sentence?

Student: Some people think they are omniscient.

You: Good. Now we use the word bus, which is an abbreviation for omnibus, meaning for all—you might have seen that word.

Continue with the more transparent and obvious roots, such as the following:

aud:	to hear	as in audio, auditory, audition, auditorium
cur:	to run	as in current, incur, curriculum, cursive
vert:	to turn	as in vertigo, invert, convert, introvert, extrovert
pend:	to hang	as in pendant, pendulum, depend, impend, suspend
tract:	to drag	as in tractor, distract, abstract, contract, detract
vene:	to come	as in convene, intervene, adventure, advent
pute:	to think	as in compute, dispute, reputation, impute
sect:	to cut	as in section, intersect, dissect
leg:	law	as in legal, legislate, illegal
terra:	earth	as in terrain, territory, terracotta, territorial, terracotta (earthenware pottery)

Never Too Late. Diana Hanbury King. WVCED.com.

Vocabulary is an important factor in comprehension, and you should continue practicing these roots in a variety of ways. You can make cards with the root on one side and the key word and meaning on the other and use them for practice drill. You can play memory, sometimes called concentration.

Once I was watching a teacher with a group of seventh and eighth graders. While she worked on reading with half of her class, the remaining six were engaged in a game of memory. They had spread out cards on the table with the roots and meanings on the side facing down. They were taking turns trying to find a match and gain a pair.

The lunch bell rang. The teacher said, "Lunch time." The group ignored her and kept on playing.

"Lunch. Didn't you hear the bell?" she said.

The rest of the class started to leave. The teacher said, "You guys had better leave or there won't be any food left."

One of them spoke up forcefully, "Okay, but PROMISE you won't touch our cards."

For further resources and creative ways of engaging students in learning roots, see the appendix.

Never Too Late. Diana Hanbury King. WVCED.com.

Introducing the Greek Elements 14

"It is not how I say it; it is how I write it that makes me think."   *David*

At some point you will want to work on the 11% of the language that is Greek in origin. Greek is the language of science, medicine, and even of new inventions, such as Xerox. Like Latin, Greek words are basically phonetic, and relatively easy to read and spell. But first you have to know about some unusual spellings of sounds.

Teach the following.

The /k/ sound is usually spelled ch as in the following.
Christmas, school, chrome, anchor, chemical, chaos, chorus

(In long words it can be k as in kinetic, kilogram, kaleidoscope.)

The /f/ sound is spelled ph as in the following.
phone, photo, elephant, photosynthesis, phylum, physical

Both short and long i are represented by y.
cryptic, gym, physic, style, psychology, phylum, biology, python, Olympus

There are some peculiar spellings that begin with silent letters.
psychic, pseudonym, psalm, psychology, pneumonia, mnemonic

Never Too Late. Diana Hanbury King. WVCED.com.

In Greek words the letter x is pronounced like /z/.
Xerox (xero means dry), xenophobia, Xerxes, xenophile, xylem, xylophone, xeroculture (the part of your garden where the hose can't reach)

Unlike Latin roots, which are mostly verbs, Greek roots are mostly nouns. We call them elements, and words are often formed by two elements and often connected by the letter o. Introduce them in the same way that you did the Latin roots, by engaging your student in talking about them.

Here are some to get you started.

You: Acro is a Greek root that means high. What do you think acrophobia might mean?
Student: Being scared of heights?
You: Right. And how would you explain acrobat?
Student: Maybe a person who jumps high.
You: Yes, or a trapeze artist. The Greeks built a temple to their gods called the Acropolis. Where do you think they placed it?
Student: On a high hill?
You: Now let's Google it and you will see! [Or you could produce a picture.]

You: What do firefighters get by hooking up to a hydrant?
Student: Water.
You: Right. And where do you think a hydroplane lands?
Student: On water.
You: Yes. Now, I grow hydrangeas in my garden. What do you think they need a lot of?
Student: Water?
You: Of course. If you don't drink enough in hot weather, what do you suffer from?
Student: Dehydration. [If the student doesn't know, you might say, "Use the prefix de-."]

Never Too Late. Diana Hanbury King. WVCED.com.

You: An old word for rabies is hydrophobia. Why do you think it was called that?

Student: An animal scared of water?

You: Apparently, though I have never seen a rabid animal. Have you?

You will notice that there are often several possible combinations. For instance, phone means sound, and from it you can get phonetic, telephone, gramophone, xylophone, and others. Phobia means fear, and you can talk about claustrophobia, acrophobia, xenophobia, arachnophobia, hydrophobia, and agoraphobia.

Here are some more useful elements for you to work with:

aud:	to hear	as in audio, auditory, audition, auditorium
phil	love	philter, xenophile, philosophy, Philadelphia
ge	earth	geology, geography, geometry, geothermal
astr	star	astrology, astronomy, asterisk, aster, astronomical, astronaut
-ology	study of	biology sociology, technology
psyche	mind	psychic, psychology, psychotic, psychosis
soph	wise	philosopher, sophisticated, sophomore (The last incidentally, means "wise fool!")
auto	self	automatic, autograph, autobiography, automobile, autocrat
pyr	fire	pyre, pyromaniac, pyrometer, pyrotechnics (The last is a fancy word for fireworks.)
mono	one	monotony, monochrome, monopoly, monarch, monotone, monomial
arch	rule	monarch, anarchy, tetrarchy (Note that it is pronounced differently in archbishop and archenemy.)
poly	many	polygamy, polyglot, polygon
the	god	theology, atheist, monotheist
log	word	monologue, dialogue, catalogue

Never Too Late. Diana Hanbury King. WVCED.com.

a or an	not, none, or away	atheist, anonymous, anarchy, anemic, apostle, apostrophe
tele	distance	telephone, television, telescope, televise
hyper	overly	hyperactive, hypersensitive, hypercritical
hypo	under	hypodermic, hypoactive, hypnosis, hypothermia

Again, refer to the appendix for further resources and activities.

Never Too Late. Diana Hanbury King. WVCED.com.

The Paragraph   15

"I went to tutors. I had more tutors. I was tutored to death. That's why in my free time I am not making any appointments, other than family big dinners that you have to make." Joe was eighteen before he learned to read--not because of lack of effort on anybody's part, but because of the severity of his dyslexia, and because a lot of the teaching he had was not appropriate.

By the time your student has written hundreds of sentences, you may be ready to introduce paragraph writing. On the other hand, you might decide to start much sooner, perhaps having him dictate his ideas to you. As usual, it all depends.

While there are graphic organizers on the market, and obviously many teachers advocate their use, a better way of getting started on paragraph writing is by brainstorming and creating a list. You can aim at between ten and twenty items. You and your student might want to take turns adding things, but again you might be doing the writing. Here are some sample list topics to get you started.

things that fly	ice cream flavors
forms of transportation	excuses
farm animals	zoo animals
playground equipment	flowers
geographic features	trees

team sports	appliances
fishing equipment	tools for woodworking
kinds of housing	camping equipment
religions	laws you would like to change
ways to help the environment	favorite movies
uses for Scotch tape	ways to cook eggs
ski equipment	how to train for a marathon
things you can buy for a dollar	what you can do in 5 minutes
clothing for cold weather	kinds of weather
animals that make good pets	safety rules for children
dangerous jobs	boring things
safety rules for cyclists	uses for credit cards

Throughout the writing process, you will be guided by the life experiences and interests of your students.

Once I had occasion to work with a sullen and somewhat antagonistic teenager. He had no intention of engaging in any writing activity. I happened to know that he loved hunting, and I began by feigning ignorance and asking whether there were safety rules one had to follow when carrying a gun. Well, he was eager to enlighten me, especially as I punctuated his list of rules with questions, such as, "Why would you bother to unload your gun just because you are climbing over a fence?" and "Why would you care which way the gun is pointing as long as your finger is not on the trigger?" We ended up developing a paragraph of which he was obviously proud.

Whatever ideas your student offers, be interested and respectful. You can also explain that writing is a thinking exercise, never a test of spelling.

There are several steps in transforming a list into a basic paragraph.

You could start with the title, which might be the heading of the list. Note

63

Never Too Late. Diana Hanbury King. WVCED.com.

that your own titles are never underlined and that the first word and all the important words are capitalized.

Then mark at least three items on the list that you would like to use and change each one into a sentence. These will be called the supporting sentences for the paragraph. Start with them because they are the easiest part of the paragraph to compose. You might practice this activity for a while before going on to talk about the topic sentence.

Next, formulate a topic sentence. The topic sentence is the most difficult part of the sentence to compose. It tells what the sentence is about and may include the title. Here are some examples.

There are several safety rules that you should teach your young child.
I have experienced a number of narrow escapes.
Everyone should try to protect our fragile environment.

Finally, you need a concluding sentence to wrap things up. This can express your judgment, your feeling, your advice, or your solution to a problem. Again, here are some examples.

Never go camping without the proper equipment.
Everyone should endeavor to recycle things that need not go to waste.
When you travel, plan to arrive at the airport at least two hours before your flight takes off.
Unfortunately global warming is now inevitable.

It may be useful to create a worksheet for the first few paragraphs your student writes. It could look something like this:
Title
Topic sentence
Support #1
Support #2
Support #3
Conclusion

Never Too Late. Diana Hanbury King. WVCED.com.

You do need at least three supporting sentences, but you can have more.

The easiest kind of paragraph to compose is the example paragraph. When you are organizing this paragraph, you will arrange the ideas from least to most important. The same applies to the reason paragraph. Of course when you write a process or "how-to" paragraph, you will list the steps in order.

Your student should write lots of these basic five-sentence paragraphs as they provide practice in thinking and planning that will be essential to the more advanced kinds of writing, as well as begin to impact his comprehension skills. Now, when he is reading expository or textbook material, you can begin to challenge him as to what the writer is up to. Is she giving examples or reasons? Is she classifying? Is she explaining the steps or stages in a process? Is she comparing or contrasting? Is she trying to persuade the reader to think or act in some way?

The next step is to teach the expanded paragraph. You can select one of the basic paragraphs your student has already composed and ask him to develop his ideas further by giving more information about each one of his supporting sentences. At this point you will also introduce transition words that signal that one point is finished and the next is coming up. At first, you can teach him three useful all-purpose ones: first, next, and finally or lastly. Later, as he gains experience with the different forms of exposition, you can introduce others for variety. A chart listing the various transition words might be a good thing to have on your wall or in his notebook.

The final step will be to turn the expanded paragraph into an essay. (See Chapter 18.)

Never Too Late. Diana Hanbury King. WVCED.com.

A Diversion   16

"So it is a matter of survival. You have to excel at what you can do and avoid what you can't."   Brian

 When I was teaching in Dunnabeck, the summer program I used to run in Pennsylvania, one day a student who had overheard my teaching approached me. He said, "I wish you could be my tutor."

I was surprised, because in those days I was very strict and demanding— thankfully, I have mellowed with age.

So, I asked him, "Why on earth would you want me?"

He said, "It's all those stories you tell."

I thought, "Me? Waste precious time telling stories during a tutoring session!" And then I realized what he was talking about. I could never pass up an interesting etymology.

Word origins are often intriguing. Try to weave them into your teaching as the occasion arises. You might have a moment at the end of your lesson, or perhaps the weather is wet and cold and your student not in the best of moods.

Never Too Late. Diana Hanbury King. WVCED.com.

I have often introduced the subject of word origins by talking about surnames. For a long time in England and Europe too, people were known by their first names only. As there were in any village people with the same name, they were most often distinguished one from another in one of four ways:

#1 The name of their father. Johnson, Jackson, Thompson, Peterson, Jefferson. In Scotland by the prefix Mac- or Mc- in MacDonald, McGee, and in Ireland by the prefix O', as in O'Malley, or O'Leary. Fitz, from Norman French, meant son as in FitzWilliam or FitzPatrick. In Arabic, *ibn* means "son of." Russian has two suffixes: *ovich* means son of and *ovna* means daughter of.

#2 Some feature of their appearance: Short, Young, Stout, Strong, Long (meaning tall), Black, White, Brown (a reference to hair or skin color). Eric the Red must have been a redhead. The influx of the Vikings with their blond hair probably accounts for the frequency of the name White.

#3 Their occupation. Some of these common names refer to trades still in use, such as Cook, Baker, Gardener, Taylor, Potter, Carpenter, Smith, Seaman, Farmer, and others to trades no longer familiar to us, such as Archer, Wainwright (a person who makes wagons or carts), Fletcher (an arrow maker), Cooper (a barrel maker), Bailiff or Bailey (a steward). In the Middle Ages, armor needed constant repair and attention, with the result that Smith is a common name not just in England, but on the continent as in German Schmidt and Spanish Herero. Names such as King, Prince, or Earl do not mean that your ancestors held lofty positions, but that they served the nobility and were known as, for instance, the King's man.

#4 Their place of origin or dwelling. Often this is a geographical feature, such as Hill, River, Lake, Meadow, Wood, Bridge, Churchill.

Never Too Late. Diana Hanbury King. WVCED.com.

Surnames did not become mandated in England until after the Norman Conquest and the introduction of the poll tax. By the end of the fourteen hundreds, surnames were required on all legal documents. However, it is still possible to trace the original meaning or etymology of many common names. One of my favorites is a girl with the surname Hoar—one of her ancestors must have been blond. She played on a coeducational soccer team. When they played against other schools, you can imagine the delight members of her team took when calling out her name!

My father's name was Hanbury, originally meaning High Hill. My mother's name Rawnsley originally meant Raven's Law and is of Scandinavian origin. I married James King.

There are many excellent sources with lists of interesting word origins (cf. Resources). One of these, John Ayto's *Dictionary of Word Origins*, has interested my students so much that it disappeared from my library. A colleague of mine told me her copy too had vanished.

Here are 20 of my favorites to get you started:

petrify	to change to stone (Latin)
sophomore	wise fool (Greek)
muscle	little mouse (flex your muscle and you'll see) (Latin)
fizzle	to fart softly (Old English)
disaster	against the stars (Latin)
tadpole	toad head (Old English)
hippopotamus	river horse (Greek)
bonfire	bone fire (from the time of the plagues) (Old English)
curfew	cover the fire (French)
avocado	testicle (Nahuahl)
gypsy	from Egypt where they were thought to originate
leotard	from Jules Leotard, a French acrobat
boycott	from the mean Irish landlord, Captain Boycott

Never Too Late. Diana Hanbury King. WVCED.com.

meander	winding, from the Greek river by that name.
candidate	in Rome those running for office wore white
sandwich	from the earl who invented it so that he would not have to interrupt his card game
gymnasium	naked (the Greeks exercised naked)
silhouette	from the inventor, Etienne de Silhouette
guy	from Guy Fawkes who was caught trying to blow up the House of Parliament and is still burned in effigy in England every Fifth of November.
lunatic	from the French for moon. If the moon shone on you while you slept, it might steal your wits away.

Never Too Late. Diana Hanbury King. WVCED.com.

"I don't know what I enjoy most, the hunt or the table, the fishing or the sushi. I get so much fun out of both. One thing I have learned is that I really wasn't set up for the office. That routine drove me to drink." Brian

Reading comprehension is a complicated process with many factors.

In the first place, if students cannot read the words, there is no way they can comprehend the material, although some of them are incredibly skilled at understanding material even if there are many words they cannot read. This ability can lead to misdiagnosis, as silent reading tests may not be an accurate measure of his skill. So, obviously the first step in remediation is to work at decoding skills in the manner described in this text.

Then a weak vocabulary is another factor. When most of us engage in daily conversation, we use a limited vocabulary. Students who do not learn to read are exposed to fewer words. The work with Greek and Latin based words described in this text is the most efficient way of developing a higher-level vocabulary.

One suggestion I have made in this book is to spend time reading to your students. You can start with simple, short things such as Aesops fables, folk tales, or mythology. Then go on to follow your student's interests. If he is interested in a sport, in art, in cars, planes, or trains, in history, or in a craft, then that is what he might like to learn about.

Talking about what you are reading is vital. If you are reading fiction, you would start by establishing the setting, the time and place where the action takes place. Then you might want to list the characters as they enter the story. As the plot unfolds, you can engage him in guessing what might come next and in predicting the outcomes. You can teach the various parts of a plot (i.e., exposition, rising action, climax, falling action, and denouement - not necessarily using these terms). *Stone Fox*, *Of Mice and Men*, *The Pearl*, and some of O'Henry's stories are possibilities with which I have found success.

Teaching about metaphorical language is important. Working with proverbs or with poetry provides opportunities to develop this skill. Very often finding the theme, in other words not just what the book is about, but what it means, takes practice and experience in reading. Some of Aesop's Fables might work in developing this skill.

If on the other hand you are reading non-fiction or expository material, your approach will be different. As she learns the various kinds of expository writing briefly introduced in this text, she will be able to pick out topic sentences, main ideas, and supporting details. She should be able to tell whether the writer is giving examples, providing reasons, classifying, persuading, comparing or contrasting, or even describing a situation, telling a story, or relating an experience that makes a point. There is no doubt that practice in expository writing improves comprehension, especially of textbook material.

SQ3R, a technique introduced by Francis Pleasant Robinson in his 1946 text *Effective Study*, may prove useful for your students, especially when they are using textbooks. Instruct them in the four steps as follows.

* * *

71

Never Too Late. Diana Hanbury King. WVCED.com.

#1 **Survey**: Flip through the chapter looking at headings, illustrations, and diagrams or charts.

#2 **Question**: Ask yourself what you expect to learn from the chapter. If there are questions at the end of the chapter, you might begin to think about them so that you will be on the lookout for any relevant information.

#3 **Read**: Read through the chapter.

#4 **Recite**: Repeat the information out loud.

#5 **Review**. Review the information, perhaps while you are doing something else – cleaning up the kitchen, raking leaves or going for a walk, driving to school, or gardening. Going over the information in your mind just before you fall asleep is another possibility that works well for some people.

You might choose to take the chapter one section at a time, rather than tackle the whole thing at once. You could take a break and drink a cup of coffee or a glass of water before resuming reading.

In some situations, the reader might have to learn to continue reading in order to learn the meaning of a word. For instance, study the following passage:

He suffered from acrophobia with the result that his job of climbing ladders and setting stage lights was always a challenge. He never lost his fear of heights.

Of course, intelligence is a factor in reading comprehension. However, do not necessarily rely on a report of a low IQ. There are many reasons why this might be an inaccurate report. If indeed you are working with a person

Never Too Late. Diana Hanbury King. WVCED.com.

of limited intelligence, never forget that even a beginning reading level is far better than no reading at all. Adjust your expectations accordingly, but remember not to assume that a student cannot handle a concept until you have tried it. Over my career of teaching, I have encountered a number of students who exceeded everybody's initial predictions.

Never Too Late. Diana Hanbury King. WVCED.com.

The Essay   18

"How come I spell the word correctly today and tomorrow I get it wrong?"
David

Depending on his occupation, your student may or may not be required to write essays. On the other hand, his job might include the responsibility of writing reports. Even if the report is to be delivered orally, knowing how to organize ideas in essay format will be a valuable asset.

The easiest way to begin teaching essay writing is to start with an expanded paragraph, perhaps one your student has already written.

In going from the expanded paragraph to the essay, there are three major changes that have to be made. First of all, the topic sentence will be transformed into the introductory paragraph with perhaps three sections. Secondly, the concluding sentence will be expanded into a full-length paragraph. Finally, each of the supporting ideas will become a full-length paragraph.

Opening Paragraph
There are several ways of constructing the Opening Paragraph, but here is a formula that has worked for my students. Teach that the opening paragraph has three parts.

#1. Opening statements designed to attract the attention of the reader. These could take the form of one or more questions, e.g. "What do you think happens to objects we recycle?" or "When did people realize the earth was round not flat?" Perhaps a statement that is the opposite of the point you plan to make, e.g. "Most teachers are overpaid, " or "Surely there is no such thing as climate change." You could use a quotation, e.g. "The future belongs to those who believe in the beauty of their dreams" (Eleanor Roosevelt), or "If you can't stand the heat, get out of the kitchen." (Harry Truman). It might be an interesting fact, such as "The Vikings invented freeze-dry," or "Light travels at 186,000 miles a second.

It might start with an anecdote, such as the following: "I had finished a country picnic with a couple of my friends when I was horrified to see one of them chuck his empty beer bottle against a rock. This was in the days before recycling, but as I made him pick up the pieces of glass, I pointed out the fact that not only was he littering the countryside, but sun shining through the broken glass could even start a fire in the dry grass."

In reading magazines or newspapers, you will notice that this last technique is often used by professional writers.

 #2. The thesis statement-- the equivalent of the topic sentence in a paragraph. This is the most important part of the opening paragraph and needs to state clearly and precisely the argument that the essay intends to make.

#3. The plan. This is a long sentence, or a series of short sentences, that lists in order the points that support the thesis statement. In this way the writer can keep things in order. Just as in a paragraph, the supporting ideas will usually be arranged from least to most important.

Supporting paragraphs
Each one of these will begin with a topic sentence and will follow the

Never Too Late. Diana Hanbury King. WVCED.com.

same construction as those written in expanded paragraphs. They will add details and provide further information. Often, the paragraphs will be linked with such phrases as another example, yet another reason, a more important reason, yet another instance, and the most important reason. Each paragraph will have a concluding sentence. Except in the case of compare/contrast essays (in which case you may have one paragraph about each thing being compared, or two paragraphs--one for similarities and one for differences), you need at least three supporting paragraphs.

Concluding Paragraph

The conclusion, rather than being a single sentence, now has two parts. First comes the summary, which can be several sentences in length, and restates the supporting points. Then comes the conclusion, which might be a piece of advice, or a solution to a problem,

Never Too Late. Diana Hanbury King. WVCED.com.

Technology 19

Many years ago I called Tim, a former student of mine, to congratulate him on being able to start college. I asked if he was finding the advent of spellcheck had helped him with his writing. "Diana," he said, "my spelling never went out of the third grade. I have no use for that thing!"

Since that time there have been significant advances in technology. Even fourth graders are being issued iPads. By high school, assignments are given and turned in online. College courses no longer require paper textbooks. There are portable devices that will read anything—even the menu in a restaurant. There are excellent speech-to-text programs that are a godsend for some. Hardcopy versions of reference books, including encyclopedias, thesauruses, and dictionaries, are no longer needed. In fact, libraries will no longer accept donations of the World Books you purchased for your children. The OED is now available only online. These are tremendous advances that in many ways have leveled the playing field for students because the resources are available to all. And, of course, for the dyslexic, the right program can be a real lifesaver.

On the other hand, children do still need to learn to read and write. There is interesting research that indicates that students who take lecture notes by hand remember and understand better; that handwriting, as opposed to keyboarding, engages more neurons in the brain and results in greater creativity; and finally that reading from a book, rather than a screen, increases comprehension and recall significantly.

Never Too Late. Diana Hanbury King. WVCED.com.

Jamie Martin is a nationally known expert on technology for students with dyslexia and may be reached at atdyslexia.com. He believes that ideally remediation and accommodation should go hand-in-hand. He is convinced that the two approaches have a symbiotic relationship. Technology use is improved when a dyslexic's language skills get better, and certain language skills can get a boost from carefully selected technology. For example, speech-to-text is a more efficient method of writing when the writer can decode the words being printed on the screen. Another example involves reading comprehension. When dyslexics struggle with decoding, text-to-speech tools can allow tutors to focus on comprehension strategies with texts that are appropriate for their students' intellectual levels. In short, we should not be too quick to assume that technology will solve everything and that we do not need to bother teaching reading and writing skills. In this day and age, both are important to the success of people with dyslexia.

Learning touch-typing is important and can be done at any age. For one thing, not only is it faster, but unlike hunt-and-peck, it imprints correct spelling in the brain. The quickest and most efficient way to learn it is through the Alphabetic Method, which I developed years ago. (See Resources in the appendix.) Roger Saunders, a nationally respected psychologist who was known to many of us for his work with dyslexia, used to say, "Keyboarding offers a whole new opportunity to learn spelling." He himself was a fairly reliable speller on the keyboard, but his handwritten notes and letters were something else.

In working with adults, who are often discouraged and set in the belief that they will never become literate, the right program can make all the difference. Once they can learn to use technology, they will be more willing to invest time and effort in learning to read and write.

* * *

Never Too Late. Diana Hanbury King. WVCED.com.

Here are Jamie's suggestions for assistive technology resources:

Noodle.com (Assistive Technology Articles):
https://www.noodle.com/topics/assistive-technology/articles

Understood.com (Assistive Technology Section):
https://www.understood.org/en/school-learning/assistive-technology

Wrightslaw.com (Assistive Technology Section):
http://www.wrightslaw.com/info/atech.index.htm

"I know that word must exist. If not, it should."
"How do you think you spell it?"
"No, just tell me."   David

Expository writing, or exposition, is writing that explains. It does not tell a story, nor does it usually describe. Textbooks and manuals are forms of exposition. Knowledge of the kinds of exposition will enable your student to write more clearly and to understand textbooks. It will certainly improve his reading comprehension. There are several kinds of exposition.

1. **Example**: The simplest is simply a list. For instance, you could write about people who wear uniforms, kinds of weather, interesting jobs, junk foods, building materials, toys, or things to do at the beach or the mall.

2. **Process**: The next thing is how to do something. For instance, how to help the environment, how to make a peanut butter and jelly sandwich, how to get a driver's license, how to stay fit, how to hang a picture, or how to cook something.

3. **Reason** is a little more difficult: You can write about why you should vote for a certain candidate, why it is important to avoid pesticides, why people should learn a second language, or why the drinking age should be changed.

4. **Persuasion** is simply a jazzed up reason paragraph, written with a particular audience in mind. For instance, you might want to persuade your boss that you deserve a raise or shorter working hours, your son that he needs to start saving money, your friend that she should quit smoking, or your neighbors that they should contribute to the local food pantry.

5. There are three ways of doing **comparison/contrast**. The simplest is to write all about one, then all about the other. Next, is to list differences and similarities in separate paragraphs. The most advanced is to describe each point by point. In the latter the two things being compared are always listed in the same order. This is the technique best used for complicated subjects, for instance comparing two cities, two colleges, two careers, two systems of government, or two resorts.

"'You need to change from college prep to general ed because you'll never make it in college,' is what they told me." Gary ignored this advice and went on to graduate with a major in elementary education. He is still teaching.

Word Play

English prepositions are often attached or paired to words with changes of meaning, and often becoming abstract rather than literal, or transparent.

Over and **under** is one such pair. The meaning of an overpass—sort of a bridge—and an underpass—a tunnel—is transparent as is undertow and undermine. And perhaps, over- or underpaid. Underwear is obvious, as is overcoat. You might buy something that is overpriced. On the other hand, overlook is not the same as look over, and oversee has the meaning of supervise.

On and **off** is another pair. Put off is to postpone, but off putting means obnoxious. You can put on airs, and put on a brave face. You can go on and off a highway by the on and off ramps. An ongoing debate means it is not over yet. If something is on and off, it means it is not happening all the time, such as a romance.

And then there is **in** and **out**. An outlook is not the same as a lookout. People can be insiders or outsiders. The ins and outs of something can mean the basics. If you look into something, you may be investigating.

Life can have its **ups** and **downs**. You can download a program, and you can load up on groceries. Downbeat is a musical term, but if you are upbeat you are optimistic, and downhearted means depressed. If you downplay something, you do not give it importance. If you are up and about, you are ready to begin your day, but if you are down and out, you may be homeless. Downright means extremely, as in "He was downright rude to me." Uptight means tense and nervous. You can put up with something, and if you are up to something you may be planning mischief.

Some of these expressions are idioms.

Idioms
An idiom is an expression that does not mean what it seems to mean. For instance, "It was raining cats and dogs" simply means that it was pouring.

Here are a few interesting idioms that do not mean what they seem to mean. Talk about what they really mean, and then perhaps think of situations where they might apply.

a loose cannon	a wild goose chase
a pain in the neck	turn over a new leaf
turn a blind eye to	takes the cake
bats in the belfry	go bananas
other fish to fry	have the upper hand
heard it through the grapevine	went to pot
sour grapes	take it with a grain of salt
see the light	kept in the dark
lost her head	on my bucket list

Never Too Late. Diana Hanbury King. WVCED.com.

Symbolic Language

A symbol is something that stands for something besides itself. Everyone is familiar with flags as symbols of countries and of crosses and crescents as symbolizing religions. Mathematical symbols stand for processes or concepts, such as infinity.   Arrows mean directions.

Colors can be symbols. Black is associated with death and mourning—though in China yellow is the color of mourning. Light can be a symbol of knowledge or enlightenment.   A clever person is said to be "bright." Darkness can mean ignorance, as "He was kept in the dark." In heraldry, green symbolized jealousy, and we still use the expression, "green with envy." Nowadays green symbolizes natural things that do not harm the planet. Singing the blues can mean sorrow. Red means danger of some sort, as a stoplight.   Also note, "Red sky in the morning, sailor's warning." "Red as a beet," signifies embarrassment. If you see red, you are angry.

Similes and metaphors are comparisons that symbolize things in a way. Similes use like or as to connect.

sly as a fox	slippery as an eel
quiet as a mouse	sharp as a tack
strong as an ox	gentle as a lamb
brave as a lion	drinks like a fish
sleeps like a log	passed out like a light

Metaphors make comparisons more directly, without using like or as. What do we mean when we say, "The place was a zoo?"

What do these mean?

America is a melting pot.	Time is money.
He is a night owl.	My dad is a road hog.
She's a couch potato.	The assignment was a breeze.

Never Too Late. Diana Hanbury King. WVCED.com.

He's a chicken.   You are an angel.
The Lord is my shepherd.

You might read the Robert Frost poem, "The Road Not Taken," and discuss the meaning of roads as used in the poem. Other short poems relatively easy to read and discuss are "Mother to Son," by Langston Hughes, "Hope is The Thing With Feathers," by Emily Dickinson, and "A Red, Red, Rose," by Robert Burns.

Popular song lyrics are another possible source: "Hound Dog," by Elvis Presley, "Life is a Highway," by Rascal Flatts, "Heart of Gold," by Neil Young, "The Dance," by Garth Brooks," and "I'm Already There," by Lone Star.

As always, be guided by what interests and engages your student.

Words with More than One Meaning
English contains many short words that have several meanings. Discussing these can be an engaging activity. You could take turns with your student naming meanings and perhaps suggest that in future lessons, he might come up with one to be added to the list. Here are some easy ones to start with:

bat, pen, skip, date, fast, roll, tie, air, arm

The dialogues might go as follows:

You: The word nut has several meanings.
Student: What you eat?
You: Yes. And what might you find in a workshop?
Student: Nuts and bolts?
You: Yes. And what if a person is nuts?
Student. Crazy.

Never Too Late. Diana Hanbury King. WVCED.com.

You: What if we say, "He's nuts about that girl?"
Student: He really adores her!

You: We just mentioned bolt, as in nuts and bolts. Think of any other possibilities?
Student: No…
You: What if we say, "She was in a hurry and bolted her sandwich?"
Student: Ate it fast.
You: Yes. What if a horse bolts?
Student: It runs fast?
You: Yes. And how about a lightning bolt?
Student: Of course.

You: What comes to mind with bat?
Student: Baseball.
You: Anything else?
Student: I can't think of anything.
You: How about the animal that flies around at dusk.
Student: Of course!
You: What if I were to say, "She is bats?"
Student: Crazy.
You: It is really short for "bats in the belfry." A belfry is a tower on a church where they hang the bells. The expression meant having bats flying around in one's head.
Student: Interesting.

More possibilities:
deck, die, file, wax, log, head, fire, rock, corn, pick, cold, pot, switch, net, slip, cast

Synonyms, Antonyms, and Homonyms

Synonyms are words that mean the same thing. For instance, you can probably think of many words that mean to speak, to go, or to be afraid or angry.

Antonyms are words with opposite meanings, such as slow/fast, hot/cold, yes/no, or pro/con. Sometimes the change is made by adding a prefix or a suffix, e.g., lucky/unlucky, sane/insane, or hopeful/hopeless.

Homonyms, or homophones, are words that sound the same, but are spelled differently. There are many of these, and they cause problems for spelling, which can best be solved by inventing mnemonic devices, e.g., I hear with my ear, and here and there.

Maybe you can invent ways of remembering some of the following common ones:
mail/male, seem/seam, reed/read, mane/main, wood/would, tow/toe, sun/son, fare/fair, bear/bare, sale/sail, stair/stare, pail/pale, ail/ale, raise/raze, teem/team, beet/beat, reign/rain

Some of these homophones are addressed in the spelling mnemonics decks mentioned in the appendix of this text.

Euphemisms

The Greek prefix eu means good, and a euphemism is a polite way of saying something we may not want to mention.

For instance, instead of saying a person has died, we might say, "he passed away" or just, "he passed." Again, a restroom is not where we go to rest. Other terms are "Ladies or Gents," "Mens or Womens." In England it is called the loo. In Victorian times, legs, ankles, and of course breasts were considered unmentionable. Instead of referring to chicken parts as "legs" or "breasts," they became "light or dark meat." And of

Never Too Late. Diana Hanbury King. WVCED.com.

course, there are many euphemisms for sex organs, as well as for what we do with them.

Onomatopoeia
This is a very fancy word for words that imitate sounds; they are often found in comic books. Here are some examples though I expect you can come up with others:

boom, crash, bang, pop, zoom, glug, gulp, pow, swish, flop, plop

Palindromes
A palindrome is a word that is spelled the same forwards and backwards. They include proper noun examples, such as Eve and Otto and the following: level, madam, civic, kayak, racecar, radar, refer, solos.

The following are palindrome sentences--the first referring to Napoleon's exile:
Able was I ere I saw Elba.
A man, a plan, a canal, Panama.
Never odd or even.
Dammit, I'm mad.

Synechdoche
This means an expression where the part can stand for the whole. "All hands on deck" or "Many hands make light work," do not just mean hands; they mean people. Here are several more:

    counting heads to make sure nobody is missing
    boots on the ground (meaning soldiers)
    arm of the law (meaning police)

Perhaps you can think of others.

Conclusion 22

David was 22 when he learned to read in 1978. Thirty years later, this is what he wrote about the experience:

"It was the twin silences that I remember the most, the silence of the room where I was working, and the silence of my mind not yet receiving. Then like the sun appearing after the clouds have parted, light flooded my brain as I heard the thoughts of another inside the silence of my head. The ropes of the fisherman cut his hands as he pulled the fish in, as he strained against the ropes and his feet pushed against the gunnel of the boat, tears fell on my face as I realized that he shared these thoughts, his deep emotions with me, he cared enough to place them on paper. And this teacher had taught me how to glean these words alive, alive in my brain, the silence, and the stillness. How wonderful! This is what I felt when you taught me to read The Old Man and the Sea."

Never ever forget, your student has a long history of failure and disappointment behind him. He has certainly been called lazy, stupid, and careless, and may have been shamed and punished by his teachers and teased and even bullied by his peers. Even if his teachers were kind, understanding, and well meaning, they may not have known how to help him learn to read. He has always believed that it was his fault that he failed to learn. The wonder is that he is still willing to try to learn and to trust you to teach him. Treat him with respect.

Never Too Late. Diana Hanbury King. WVCED.com.

As to what to do next, if you ask any experienced therapist, the answer you will get is invariably, "It depends." And indeed it does. Certainly you will want to vary the activities and to keep in mind Anna Gillingham's wise dictum, "Go as fast as you can, but as slowly as you must."

If you do it right, you will be privileged to have transformed a life.

Never Too Late. Diana Hanbury King. WVCED.com.

Recommended Resources

Phonology, Syllables & Syllabication

King, Diana Hanbury & Karen Leopold. *Conquering Spelling Demons*, Level 1 & 2. Spelling mnemonics decks that help children with non-phonetic and easy-to-confuse words. wvced.com.

Van Cleave, William. *Basic Sound Deck*. Drill cards for reading and spelling of basic sounds and symbols. Cards include keywords and place of articulation. Keywords match with Van Cleave's *Everything* text.

Van Cleave, William. *Basic Phonics Concept Charts*. Ready reference color visuals, including syllable patterns, vowel teams, and more. wvced.com.

Van Cleave, William. *Everything You Want To Know & Exactly Where To Find It*. Orton-Gillingham based reference guide covering concepts and extensive word lists. Begins with basic phonics concepts and moves through advanced word structure. wvced.com.

Van Cleave, William & Caroline Dover. *Phrases & Sentences for Reading & Spelling*. Phrases and sentences organized by phonetic concept for both reading and spelling dictation; companion to the *Everything* text. wvced.com.

Van Cleave, William. *Sorters*. Three-pocket sorts covering a variety of concepts. Shuffle the cards, and ask children to sort by concept. wvced.com.

Oral Reading

Listed in order of difficulty from easiest to more challenging:
Gardiner, John Reynolds. *Stone Fox*.
Gannett, Ruth Styles. *My Father's Dragon* and others in the series.
DiCamillo, Kate. *The Tale of Despereaux*, *The Miraculous Journey of Edward Tulane*, *Tiger Rising*.

Never Too Late. Diana Hanbury King. WVCED.com.

Doahl, Roald. *Charlie and the Chocolate Factory*, *Danny, The Champion of the World*, and *James and the Giant Peach*.

White, E.B. *Charlotte's Web*.

Steinbeck, John. *The Pearl*.

Lai, Thanhha. *Inside Out and Back Again*.

Steinbeck, John. *The Red Pony* and *Of Mice and Men*.

Hemingway, Ernest. *The Old Man and the Sea*.

Dahl, Roald. *Going Solo*.

Writing Skills

King, Diana. *Cursive Writing Skills* (left- and right-handed versions). Designed for the older student. epsbooks.com.

King, Diana. *Keyboarding Skills*. Revolutionary method of instructing students in keyboarding, using the methodology discussed in the motor component chapter of this text. epsbooks.com.

King, Diana Hanbury. *Writing Skills*, Books A, One, Two, and Three. Series of workbooks that cover sentence structure and expository writing. Book A is for 2nd-3rd graders, Book 1 is for 4th-5th graders, Book 2 is for 7th-8th graders, and Book 3 is for high school. *Teacher's Handbook* accompanies the series. epsbooks.com.

Pencil Grips. Several grip styles, available to assist students with developing good pencil grip. wvced.com.

Van Cleave, William. *Concept Cards*. Grammar terms, including definitions and examples. wvced.com.

Van Cleave, William. *Writing Matters: Developing Sentence Skills in Students of All Ages*. Thorough teacher's manual covering teaching approach, scope and sequence by grade level, concepts for instruction, and excellent reference word lists -- all at the sentence level. wvced.com.

Morphology

Ayto, John. *Dictionary of Word Origins*. Fascinating word origins to share with students in order to engage their interest in the language. amazon.com.

Donah, Sandra. *Improving Morphemic Awareness*. Useful activities for older students for developing morphemic awareness using Latin and Greek morphemes. Exercises can be done orally or in writing. wvced.com.

Never Too Late. Diana Hanbury King. WVCED.com.

Gold, Diane, Elaine Russo, Linda Wallace, and Judy Shapiro. *PS: Prefixes, Suffixes, Roots*. Excellent upper elementary and lower middle school morphology text, including words, sentences, and engaging passages for each morpheme covered. wvced.com.

King, Diana Hanbury. *English Isn't Crazy*. History of the language. proedinc.com.

Morgan, Ken. *Dynamic Roots*. Three-book morphology kit for middle and high school students; includes teacher's manual, student reader, and engaging support activities. wvced.com.

Steere, Peck, and Kahn. *Solving Language Difficulties*. Contains useful advanced material, but can be used beginning in about 5th grade. Exceptions to rules introduced along with the rules - a practice to be avoided. Useful section on Latin connectives for older students.

Van Cleave, William. *Everything You Want To Know & Exactly Where To Find It*. Orton-Gillingham based reference guide covering concepts and extensive word lists. Begins with basic phonics concepts and moves through advanced word structure. wvced.com.

Van Cleave, William. *Morphology Deck*. Large reference cards that introduce morphemes (roots and affixes) with language of origin, keyword, and word list for student reading.

Van Cleave, William & Caroline Dover. *Phrases & Sentences for Reading & Spelling*. Phrases and sentences organized by phonetic concept; companion to the *Everything* text

Selected Research

Handwriting

Berninger, V.W. (March 2013). Educating Students in the Computer Age to Be Multilingual by Hand. Commentaries (National Association of State Boards of Education), 19 (1).

Berninger, V.W. (May-June 2012). Strengthening the Mind's Eye: The Case for Continued Handwriting Instruction in the 21st Century. Principal, 28-31.

Freedman, S. (Jan. 19, 2005). "Back to the Basics of a Legible Hand." The New York Times. Belaire, MD.

Graham.S. (Winter 2009-2010). Want to Improve Children's Writing? Don't Neglect Their Handwriting. American Educator, 20-27, 40. www.aft.org/pdfs/americaneducator/winter2009/graham.pdf.

Mueller, P.A. & Oppenheimer, D.M. (2014). The Pen Is Mightier Than the Keyboard: Advantages of Longhand Over Laptop Note Taking. Psychological Science, 25(6), 1159-1168.

Zubrzycki, J. (January 23, 2012). Summit to Make a Case for Teaching Handwriting. Education Week, 31 (Issue 18), 1,13.

Written Expression

Berninger, Virginia and Beverly J. Wolf. *Teaching Students with Dyslexia and Dysgraphia*: Lessons from Teaching and Science. Baltimore, MD: Brookes Publishing Co., 2009.

Brimo, Danielle, Kenn Apel, and Treeva Fountain. "Examining the contributions of syntactic awareness and syntactic knowledge to reading comprehension." *Journal of Research in Reading*. Oxford, UK: John Wiley & Sons, Ltd, April 2015.

Never Too Late. Diana Hanbury King. WVCED.com.

Eberhardt, Nancy Chapel & Monica Gordon-Pershey, eds. *Perspectives on Language and Literacy - Theme Issue: Syntax: Its Role in Literacy Learning.* Baltimore, MD: The International Dyslexia Association, Summer 2013.

Graham, Steve, Charles A. MacArthur, and Jill Fitzgerald, Eds. *Best Practices in Writing Instruction.* New York, NY: The Guilford Press, 2007.

Graham, Steve & Karen R. Harris. *Writing Better: Effective Strategies for Teaching Students With Learning Difficulties.* Baltimore, MD: Paul H. Brookes Publishing Co., 2005.

MacArthur, Charles A., Steve Graham, & Jill Fitzgerald. *Handbook of Writing Research.* New York, NY: The Guilford Press, 2006.

National Writing Project & Carl Nagin. *Because Writing Matters: Improving Student Writing in Our Schools.* San Francisco, CA: Jossey-Bass, 2006.

Scott, Cheryl M. "A Case for the Sentence in Reading Comprehension." *Language, Speech, and Hearing Services in Schools*, Vol. 40. 184-91. April 2009.

Troia, Gary A. "Writing Instruction for Students with Learning Disabilities." *Handbook of Writing Research.* Eds. Charles A. MacArthur, Steve Graham, and Jill Fitzgerald. New York, NY: The Guilford Press, 2006.

Morphology

Bowers, P. N., Kirby, J. R, & Deacon, S.H. 2010. "The effects of morphological instruction on literacy skills: A systematic review of the literature." *Review of Educational Research*, 80, 144–179.

Goodwin, A. P., & Ahn, S. 2010. "A meta-analysis of morphological interventions: effects on literacy achievement of children with literacy difficulties." *Annals of Dyslexia*, 60, 183–208.

Goodwin, A. P. & Ahn, S. 2013. "A Meta-Analysis of Morphological Interventions in English: Effects on Literacy Outcomes for School-Age Children." *Scientific Studies of Reading*, 1–29, 2013.

95

Never Too Late. Diana Hanbury King. WVCED.com.

Glossary

adjective - An adjective is a word that describes a noun.

adverb - An adverb is a word that describes a verb. It tells when, where, how, or under what condition the action takes place. Adverbs often end in -ly.

clause - A clause is a group of words containing a subject and a verb. There are two kinds of clauses. A main clause is a sentence and can stand alone. A subordinate clause is not a complete sentence and cannot stand alone.

closed syllable - A closed syllable ends in a consonant and is so named because the mouth is closed at the end of it. Vowels in a closed syllable are usually short.

compound sentence - A compound sentence consists of two main clauses joined by and, but, or, nor, for, yet.

consonant-le syllable - The final syllable ending in a consonant plus le (e.g., *ta-ble, lit-tle*). Actually, in this situation, the l acts as a vowel.

coordinating conjunction - The coordinating conjunctions are **and**, **but**, **or**, **nor**, **for**, **yet**. They join the two main clauses of a compound sentence.

description - Description or descriptive writing is writing that describes.

digraph - Two letters that form a single sound (e.g., sh as in *ship*).

Never Too Late. Diana Hanbury King. WVCED.com.

diphthong - A vowel sound in which the position of the mouth shifts. Diphthongs cannot be prolonged as the sound changes. For instance, if you try to prolong long /a/, /i/, or /oy/ as in boy, you end up with a long e sound. If you try to prolong the ou sound as in shout or the long u as in few, you end up with an /oo/ sound.

exposition - Exposition, or expository writing, is writing that explains. It is the most important kind of writing to teach, especially to adults.

Greek element - Greek words usually consist of two nouns, often joined by a connective o (e.g., photograph).

grapheme - A grapheme is a letter that represents a speech sound.

I.D.A. - The International Dyslexia Association holds annual meetings throughout the country and is a source of information and materials. It can be reached at eida. org.

mnemonic - A device that helps to remember something. (e.g., The mnemonic for the colors of the rainbow is Roy G. Biv. We teach would, could, and should as the "O you lucky duck!" words.

morpheme - A morpheme is a unit of meaning. All roots, prefixes, and suffixes are morphemes. For instance, dog is one morpheme, but dogs is two. Helpfulness is three morphemes. Latin words tend to be long and have several morphemes; for instance, disappointment has four.

narration - Narration or narrative writing is writing that tells a story.

noun - A noun is the name of a person, place, thing, or idea. Proper nouns are names that are capitalized; common nouns are not.

O.G.A. - The Academy of Orton-Gillingham Practitioners and Educators trains and certifies teachers in the Orton-Gillingham Approach. It is headquartered in Amenia, NY and can be reached at ortonacademy.org.

open syllable - An open syllable is a syllable that ends in a vowel. It is so named because after pronouncing a word such as no or hi, the mouth is slightly open. Vowels in an open syllable are long.

Never Too Late. Diana Hanbury King. WVCED.com.

Orton-Gillingham Approach - Originally based on the work of Anna Gillingham, this is a way of approaching teaching rather than a method. Multisensory lessons are individualized to meet the needs of each student.

predicate - The predicate of a sentence tells something about the subject and always contains the verb.

preposition - Prepositions are words that relate nouns to other nouns or to verbs (e.g., piece of cake, into the woods, from his father, before the accident). Prepositions come in phrases that begin with a preposition and end with a noun or pronoun.

pronoun - A pronoun is a word that takes the place of a noun (e.g., *we*, *they*, *that*, *which*).

r-controlled syllable - In this syllable the vowel is followed by an r that changes its pronunciation (e.g., *corn*, *farm*, *her*). In the case of double r, the vowel usually retains its pronunciation (e.g., *carry*, *sorry*).

relative pronoun - These begin subordinate clauses -- *who, whose, whom, that, which, what.*

S.O.S. - This stands for Simultaneous Oral Spelling. It is the practice of having students name each letter aloud as they form it.

stable final syllable - This is a final syllable, the spelling of which is fixed (e.g., the -ture in pic-ture, the -age in dam-age, or the -tion in na-tion).

stop - A stop is a consonant made with a single puff of air. Stopped consonants cannot be prolonged (e.g., p, b, k, t).

subject - The subject of a sentence tells who or what the sentence is about and always contains a noun or pronoun.

subordinating conjunction - A subordinating conjunction begins a subordinate clause. See the list at the end of the glossary.

Never Too Late. Diana Hanbury King. WVCED.com.

supporting sentences or paragraphs - These support the topic sentence or the thesis statement. They provide the facts or data on which the topic or thesis statement is based.

thesis statement - In an essay the thesis states the point the writer is trying to make.

topic sentence - In a paragraph the topic sentence tells what the paragraph is about.

trigraph - Three letters that form a single sound (e.g., tch as in *catch*, dge as in *edge*).

verb - A verb is a word that describes an action or a state of being. All clauses must contain a verb.

voiced/unvoiced - Voiced sounds involve the vibration of the vocal cords. You can feel the difference if you pronounce a voiced/unvoiced pair, such as p/b or g/k as you keep your hand on your throat. All vowels are voiced.

vowel-consonant-e syllable - Also known as a **silent-e** or even **magic-e** syllable. The e is silent, but the vowel preceding it is long.

vowels - Vowels, unlike diphthongs, are sounds that can be prolonged. All the short vowels are true vowels, as are long e as in *sea*, /oo/ as in *food*, *sue*, *soup*, and *grew*, and au and aw, as in *August* and *awful*.

Flip the page for subordinating conjunctions and prepositions.

Never Too Late. Diana Hanbury King. WVCED.com.

Prepositions:

Basic Prepositions

above	by	near to	through
across	close to	next to	throughout
around	down	on	to
at	far from	on top of	toward
behind	from	onto	towards
below	in	out of	under
beneath	in front of	outside	underneath
beside	inside	outside of	up
between	into	over	upon
beyond	near	past	within

Advanced Prepositions

aboard	along	except (for)	on behalf of
about	aside from	for	out
according to	atop	in addition to	prior to
after	because of	in case of	subsequent to
against	before	in place of	with
ahead of	besides	in spite of	with regard to
alongside	despite	instead of	without
among	due to	of	
amongst	during	off	

Subordinating Conjunctions:

after	because	now that	until
although	before	once	when
as	even if	since	whenever
as if	even though	so that	whether
as long as	if	than	
as soon as	in order that	though	
as though	just as	unless	

Never Too Late. Diana Hanbury King. WVCED.com.

102